THESE
ARE
THE
STORIES

Memories of a 60s Scoop Survivor

Christine Miskonoodinkwe Smith

LOS GATOS LIBRARY

LOS GATOS, CALIFORNIA

Published by Kegedonce Press
11 Park Road, Neyaashiinigmiing, ON N0H 2T0
Administration Office/Book Orders: P.O. Box 517, Owen Sound, ON N4K 5R1
www.kegedonce.com

Printed in Canada by Sotek Graphics
Art Direction: Kateri Akiwenzie-Damm
Design: Chantal Lalonde Design
Author's photo: Susan Blight
Additional photos courtesy of Christine Miskonoodinkwe Smith

Library and Archives Canada Cataloguing in Publication

Title: These are the stories : memories of a 60s Scoop survivor / Christine Miskonoodinkwe-Smith.
Names: Miskonoodinkwe-Smith, Christine, author.
Identifiers: Canadiana 20210389419 | ISBN 9781928120278 (softcover)
Subjects: LCSH: Miskonoodinkwe-Smith, Christine. | LCSH: Miskonoodinkwe-Smith, Christine—Childhood
   and youth. | LCSH: Interracial adoption—Canada. | LCSH: Indigenous children—Canada—Social
   conditions. | LCSH: Indigenous peoples—Canada—Government relations. | LCSH: Indigenous peoples—
   Cultural assimilation—Canada. | CSH: First Nations—Canada—Biography. | LCGFT: Autobiographies.
Classification: LCC HV875.7.C2 M57 2022 | DDC 362.734089/97333071—dc23

For Customer Service/Orders
Tel 1-800-591-6250 Fax 1-800-591-6251
100 Armstrong Ave. Georgetown, ON L7G 5S4
Email: orders@litdistco.ca

We acknowledge the support of the Canada Council for the Arts which last year
invested $20.1 million in writing and publishing throughout Canada.

Canada Council   Conseil des arts
for the Arts   du Canada

We would like to acknowledge funding support from the Ontario Arts Council,
an agency of the Government of Ontario.

ONTARIO ARTS COUNCIL
CONSEIL DES ARTS DE L'ONTARIO
an Ontario government agency
un organisme du gouvernement de l'Ontario

I'd like to dedicate this book to
ni mama Anna Smith,
my sisters Marguerite and Alice,
my niece Samantha,
my newly found family,
all my friends and loved ones
who have stood by me
and lastly to all Sixty Scoop survivors.

Please know I'm breaking my silence
so that you will know we are not alone.

Our voices need to be heard.

Miigwetch.

TABLE OF CONTENTS

FOREWORD

In *These are the Stories*, Christine Miskonoodinkwe Smith has collected autobiographical essays she's written over the past twenty years. Some of the essays have been published in magazines and journals. Some are being published for the first time. Together these personal stories from Christine's life provide readers with clear and painful insight into the deep, long-lasting harms caused by the Canadian child welfare system's intrusion into First Nations families and communities since the 1950s.

Prior to 1951, the Children's Aid Society (CAS) did not have jurisdiction on First Nations reserves. Outside of First Nations, the CAS had jurisdiction through provincial and territorial government authority—which did not apply on reserve. This changed in 1951 when the Indian Act (unilaterally imposed federal legislation that governs matters on reserve) was amended to allow provincial laws of general application to apply on reserve. Under section 91(24) of the British North America Act of 1867, the federal government had been given exclusive jurisdiction over "Indians and Lands reserved for Indians." Nine years later, the Indian Act was passed by the federal government of the new Dominion of Canada. The Indian Act outlined measures which controlled all aspects of the lives of First Nations people while keeping us contained on reserve lands.

Section 88 of the 1951 amendment to the Indian Act allowed "all laws of general application from time to time in force in any province [to be] applicable to and in respect of Indians in the province, except to the extent that such laws are inconsistent with this Act." One of the applications of Section 88 provided Children's Aid Societies with the authority to do their work on reserve in First Nations communities. This included taking First Nations children from their families and making them Crown Wards. For the first time, First Nations communities were under the authority of provincial child welfare laws.

At the time, the removal of First Nations children from their communities was justified as necessary, even benevolent—just as it was throughout the Indian Residential School era. Once again, the colonial government, with the assistance of allied agents, had found a way to forcibly take Indigenous children, despite the objections of First Nations and regardless of any damage that would be inflicted on the children themselves or on their families and communities. Still, the widespread abduction of First Nations children by the CAS did not happen right away. Why? The answer is simple: money. The 1951 Indian Act amendment provided jurisdiction to Children's Aid Societies but no funding to help pay the costs. It wasn't until funding agreements were put in place in 1966 that the large-scale taking of First Nations children was carried out. With provincial and territorial government jurisdiction and federal, provincial and territorial funding supporting them, Children's Aid Societies made it their mission to take First Nations children from their families and communities. The "Sixties Scoop"[1] had begun.

∗∗∗∗

Christine's essays about her life as a survivor of the Sixties Scoop encompass her earliest clear memories and continue as she works to piece together the story of who she is and what happened to her and to her family under the oppressive laws and policies of colonial, capitalist governments. Christine has spent much of her childhood and adulthood attempting to understand what led to the trauma, disruptions and experiences she endured in the early part of her life as an Indigenous person who was taken from her family, community and nation only to be bounced around a "child welfare" system that was never meant to protect Indigenous children but instead to continue the work of the Residential School system: separating Indigenous children from their families thereby disrupting familial, community and cultural bonds. The goals of both systems were never to help Indigenous families to stay together, as was their mandate otherwise. In fact, the opposite was true. The destruction of Indigenous families and communities was the intent of both systems and the deaths and harming of Indigenous children, apparently, were acceptable collateral damage in those endeavours. That vulnerable Indigenous infants and children were placed in peril physically, mentally, and spiritually did not matter—many were handed over to strangers they'd just met, strangers who were not vetted, tracked nor monitored. Some children, like Christine, were moved from place to place, separated

---

1   The term the "Sixties Scoop" was coined in 1983 by researcher Patrick Johnston, the author of the 1983 report Native Children and the Child Welfare System. Although the taking of First Nations children has not stopped, the "Sixties Scoop" is sometimes used to refer generally to the ongoing removal of Indigenous children from their homes but is mostly understood to refer to the era from the mid-1960s until the mid-1980s. The "Millenial Scoop" refers to the period from the mid 1980s to today.

from siblings, and left to deal on their own with the confusion and pain of not knowing who they were, not knowing where they belonged, and not feeling wanted or loved.

Christine's stories are sometimes triumphant, sometimes traumatic, often painful to read, and courageous of her to share. These are her stories as she remembers them. There are gaps in her stories. Or rather, there are gaps that are part of the story. Some of these gaps are the result of being taken from her family at such a young age—Christine simply doesn't know and no one has been able to fill in those missing pieces of her history. In other cases, the memories are too painful or remain buried under the weight of the mental and physical health issues that left her struggling in a haze of unhealthy coping mechanisms, prescription medications, and a cycle of hospital stays. Those memories are simply beyond reach. What Christine does remember and can tell us in these stories is both heartbreaking and enlightening and places a close up, often uncomfortable lens on the reality of life for many survivors of the Sixties Scoop. That her story is fragmented is a revealing aspect of the story itself. This is not a straightforward, linear memoir. It spirals and circles back, jumps forward and back in time, and in doing so shines a light on the darkness of Canada's mistreatment of Indigenous children.

Christine's story ultimately is a story of survival and resistance. Join her as she looks back at her journey and shares how she, as a survivor of the Sixties Scoop, has found comfort and strength in re/creating the family and community she needed and dreamed of having.

These *are* the stories.

Kateri Akiwenzie-Damm
Neyaashiinigmiing, Ontario
October 2021

Undergraduate degree graduation photo, 2016.

PREFACE

Aanii, Christine nitiishinikaas. Peguis nitoonci. Mashkedebejiki ni totem. (Hello, my name is Christine Miskonoodinkwe Smith. I am from Peguis First Nation and Buffalo is my clan.) My Anishinaabe name is Miskonoodinkwe (Red Wind Woman) which I received later in life when I returned to the teachings and language of my culture.

I am a Sixties Scoop survivor, a Bill C-31 status Anishinaabe woman and a daughter of a Saulteaux mother and a Cree father. I was born in Winnipeg forty-plus years ago. Unfortunately, my parents separated while my mother was pregnant with me. This period of time was difficult for ni mama (my mother). As a result, child welfare officials from the city stepped in and took me and three other siblings away from her. When I was three years old, my sister, Doreen Marguerite and I were adopted together into an affluent Caucasian family and brought to live in the province of Ontario.

The Canadian state has long had an assimilation practice in which large numbers of First Nations children have been removed from their families and adopted into families of non-Indigenous parents. The highest peak of adoption occurred in the '60s, '70s and early '80s and was known as the Sixties Scoop. This practice led to intense identity consequences for those who became the "product" of interracial adoption. These impacts were something the Canadian government did not care about.

Canadian policy in the twentieth century towards First Nations peoples has largely been paternalistic. Its underlying goal was to guide First Nations peoples into assimilating with Canadian ideology and practice of how Europeans wanted them to be upon first contact.

The history of adoption within First Nations communities remains a painful subject. It caused a deep and unhealed pain as it created a comprehensive assault on Indigenous families following that of sending Indigenous children to residential schools.

It is now widely accepted that First Nations children's suffering did not vanish with the closing of residential schools. This pain was carried forward inter-generationally into new circumstances and communities, if not completely different provinces (as in my case) or countries. Researchers trying to determine how many First Nations children were taken from their families during the Scoop say the task is all but impossible because adoption records from the '60s and '70s rarely indicated First Nations status (as they are now required to do). Records that are complete suggest that the adoption of First Nations children by non-Indigenous families was most pervasive in Northern Ontario and Manitoba.

As a First Nations woman who went through the '60s Scoop of Native children being removed from their families, I grew up without any knowledge of my heritage and culture, and when I was subsequently returned to the care of the Children's Aid Society at the age of ten by my emotionally, physically and spiritually abusive adoptive parents, writing became an integral part of my journey to healing and wellness. As a child, I always knew that I wanted to be a writer and that writing was my gift. I recall that when I was locked in my bedroom for hours on end, I would feverishly write poetry and short stories and slip them under my bedroom door for my sister to read.

Years later, I began writing essays to tell the story of my life. Writing these stories was part of my healing journey and when my first story "Choosing the Path to Healing" was accepted for publication in the United States in 2006 it gave me the confidence to continue with my writing.

It was while attending the University of Toronto as an undergraduate that I began receiving support and guidance from professors such as Dr. Daniel Heath Justice, Lee Maracle, and acclaimed writer Cherie Dimaline. During this time, I began freelance writing for various First Nations news outlets, doing book reviews, and writing for First Nations House in-house publication FNH magazine. In 2016, under the guidance of Cherie Dimaline, I applied for a grant through the Canada Council for the Arts for an Aboriginal Emerging Writers Residency (as it was called[2]). I was accepted and after spending two weeks in Banff Alberta learning from faculty members Kateri Akiwenzie-Damm and Gregory Scofield, I learned how to hone into a collection a selection of stories that I had written over a period of ten years. Later, I wrote more stories so that I could create a more complete narrative of my life. Because I struggle with post-traumatic stress disorder,

---

2   The term "aboriginal" is rejected by most Indigenous people in Canada, although it is still used by government and other organizations.

depression and anxiety, my recollections of some dates and details in my life are a bit foggy, but writing became my voice, and my way of saying, "I will not stay silent anymore."

In these stories, you will find repetition, the same story told again in a different way. In Indigenous storytelling, stories are often repeated; they are never just told and that's the end of them. Through repeating a story, especially when it means so much to an Indigenous person, it is a way of holding onto a thought, a memory or event.

Meeting my birth mother was a life-changing event for me, and a story I tell over and over again. It allows me to hang onto a memory of my mom because she is no longer with me in the physical world. It comforts me but also preoccupies my thoughts because I am always trying to make sense of what happened and what separated us for so many years. It's also an attempt to remember my roots and who I am.

Some of the stories in this collection were published in various First Nations news outlets, such as *Yellow Medicine Review*, *FNH Magazine*, *New Tribe Magazine*, *Native Canadian Centre* and *Anishinabek News*. A few of my stories were published in anthologies like *Growing Up Girl: Voices from Marginalized Spaces*, and websites such as *Healthy Debate* as well as others I cannot recall at this time.

It was through the writing process that I learned to find the voice I had buried out of hurt, anger and shame for so many years. To tell my stories is a way of not only healing but allowing other Sixties Scoop survivors to see that they are not alone in what they may have experienced. I hope others who have come from similar backgrounds will find their 'voices' too. We need to tell our stories so that those in power will come to know that we cannot be beaten down. We are survivors.

THESE
ARE
MY
STORIES

With my sister Marguerite (left), c. 1974.

THE BEGINNING

My childhood was not happy; in fact it was traumatic and has left me with searing emotional scars, even to this day. My adoptive home was fraught with abuse that extended beyond the emotional and mental. Physical abuse was a norm in this adoptive home and I was treated like a prisoner. My freedom was being able to attend school, but while at home I was locked in my bedroom with bolts on the door and later, to my surprise, an alarm that was also put on the doorknob of my bedroom door. If the alarm went off, the anticipation of what would happen next was terrifying. Questions would run through my mind like *Will I get a beating? Will my food be limited even more? Will I be locked inside here forever?*

I remember the first time I touched the doorknob after the alarm was installed. I had been trying to get someone to please let me out to go to the washroom. My bedroom was located on the second floor of our house and I never knew who would be walking by my room or when. It always depended on the time of the day. In this instance it was around noon on a Saturday. You've heard "out of sight, out of mind"? That's what it was like for me in my adoptive family, especially when I was locked up in my bedroom. I called many times asking to use the washroom, but no one answered me. I remember when my little hand finally reached for the doorknob and my shock when suddenly there was a piercing beeping noise emanating from my door. Immediately, fear and dread coursed through my body because I knew what was coming next—the angry footsteps coming toward my bedroom, hearing the sound of someone turning off the alarm, the sound of the bolts being fumbled with, and the door opening. I would receive a withering glare.

"You have five minutes and that's it," I'd be told.

I never had the privacy of closing the bathroom door behind me. Someone would always stand guard—that could be my adoptive father, one of three of their sons, or, sometimes, my sister. After I was finished, I would scurry back into my bedroom and listen for the door being shut and locked behind me again. I never understood what my sister and my adoptive parents' sons thought of this routine of guarding me while I was in the bathroom or what they felt was the reasoning behind the locking of the door and putting the bolts on.

My adoptive parents' sons never spoke to me, and for the majority of my time there, I was kept away from them. We lived separate lives, the kids that is, and even my adoptive parents to an extent, except for when they had to appear as a united front to the neighbours and others outside the family.

The abuse I endured extended beyond the emotional and mental aspect. It was also physical. I was deprived of a lot of foods because my adoptive parents believed that certain foods would make me fat. My sister experienced the same to a certain extent, but she never speaks about it, even to this day. These foods included carbohydrates, fried foods, baked goods, juices and soda, especially soda. The food I did eat was very carefully monitored. This monitoring of my food intake was something I carried on even after my adoptive parents gave me up. From the age of eight, I had been taught to be hyper-aware of what I could and could not put in my body. Controlling what I ate made me feel that there was at least the one thing that I could control about myself, but it also made me retreat further into myself until I was almost invisible. This need to control my diet developed into the life-threatening eating disorder, anorexia nervosa, which I struggled with from the age of twelve until my twenties.

At the age of ten, my adoptive parents, under the guise of saying I would be going to a boarding school, dropped me off at Maryvale, a home for troubled kids. While I was at Maryvale I was allowed to go for home visits with my adoptive family. I was told, "If you're good enough, maybe you can come back and live with us."

That turned out to be a lie because those home visits with my adoptive family and my sister soon stopped. I learned the true intent of being at Maryvale—I was being given up by my adoptive parents and put back into the care of the Children's Aid Society.

The Friday that I was supposed to go for a weekend visit, a staff member of Maryvale came into the lounge where I was sitting while I waited for my adoptive parents to pick me up. She looked at me, reached out, and took my hand in hers. After a couple of seconds, she said "I'm sorry, Christine, you won't be going home for a visit. In fact, your adoptive parents are returning you to the care of the Children's Aid Society, and that means you will be staying here for a while until we can find a placement for you. You will also be made a Crown ward of the Children's Aid Society."

I remember breaking down crying, and the worker sitting there, holding my hands until I willed myself to stop crying. Learning that my adoptive parents didn't want me left me beyond scarred, even though they were abusive towards me. I often felt that because they didn't want me, no one would ever want me, let alone love me. I was devastated.

I stayed in that group home for a year and then moved through three foster homes in the next seven years. The impact of being given up and moving around so much severely impacted my mental and physical health. The frequent moves reinforced my feelings of rejection and not being loved. Acting out was the only way I could feel like I was being paid attention to, even though, in retrospect, it just made people withdraw from me and made me feel lonelier.

When was eleven years old, I was placed in my first foster home. While I was there I began to run away at the slightest provocation. As a First Nations individual, I knew by my skin colour that I was different from the people I grew up around. Everywhere I lived and pretty much everyone I interacted with was non-Indigenous. At the time, it wasn't something I explored or paid much attention to. I knew it made me somewhat of an outsider, just by the way I was treated. Classmates would make fun of me, and it would just make me furious, but I kept the anger inside. That anger turned into more self-harm—cutting myself, overdosing on my medications, anything that would just take away the inner pain I was experiencing. I did not find out about being a status First Nations individual until my family doctor at the time found out I was paying for my own medication and could no longer afford it. That was when she stepped in and told me, "Indian Affairs can help you with this."

Even though I applied for my status card in order to pay for the psychiatric medications I had been put on, I didn't examine my culture any further until I moved to Toronto at the age of twenty. Acknowledging my history and my journey as an Anishinaabekwe has been difficult. It has not come naturally or easily because of all the complexities it has attached to it. All the years of searching for myself and searching for my mother and the rest of my biological family have been tiring but also rewarding. It still makes me angry and antipathetic towards the Canadian government and how they see Indigenous peoples and Indigenous children as disposable and not worth the effort to help to overcome the atrocities that have happened to us historically.

Learning my culture, traditions and the ways of my people showed me that I had every right to embrace my culture, because it had been stolen from me as a child. Despite this, my culture and traditions were embedded in me. They are a part of who I am.

With my sister Marguerite (left).

THE MISSION

I hear my sister start to whisper something, in the darkness of our bedroom. I turn towards her voice

"Christine, you gotta go to the kitchen and get us some food."

"Oh sis," I whisper back. "I don't wanna go. What if I get caught?"

"Ah, you won't get caught," my sister whispers back. "All you gotta do is tiptoe past mom and dad's room. They won't hear ya, it's late and everyone's asleep."

"Why can't you go?" I ask her. My voice turns to a whine.

"Because you're good at it, and I'm not," she replies.

I'm lying there in my twin bed with my Holly Hobbie blanket pulled up to my chin, listening to my stomach rumble. I hear the familiar growl of my sister's stomach, and know my sister is hungry too.

"Fine! I'll go," I say.

I'm on a mission. My sister and I were feeling really hungry because for some reason we had not been given very much food that day. With the sound of our stomachs growling in my ears, I am determined to get us something to eat. There is a trick to making it from our bedroom at the end of the hallway, past our parent's bedroom, and down the carpeted creaky stairs and to the fridge. I have to be as quiet as possible and not wake anybody.

The cold air hits me as I throw my blanket off and swing my feet over the edge of my bed. I throw my pink housecoat over my nightie and stand up. I try to orient myself because our bedroom only has a small nightlight and not much light emanates from it. I cross the floor quickly and open our bedroom door. Leaving the room, I catch a quick glimpse of the Holly Hobbie poster hanging by the door. That is my favorite poster. Turning from the door, I feel the carpet beneath my bare feet. It tickles my toes. It is a shag carpet and when you walk on it, your foot leaves an imprint. My feet don't. I barely weigh fifty pounds.

I creep down the hallway, dragging my fingers along the wall to help guide me through the darkness. Slowly making my way down the hallway, I notice that the door to the bathroom is slightly open, and the dim light makes it less scary for me. A couple of seconds later, I am at the top of the stairway and I take a moment to look around me. I'm right in front of my parent's bedroom, and my heart speeds up. I can hear them snoring on the other side of the bedroom door.

I take a deep breath and my little shoulders tighten. I take my first step onto the stairs and realize there's no turning back. CREAK! I pull my foot back quickly. DANG! I forgot about that stair. I make a quick leap to the small and narrow ledge above the stairs and find myself balancing precariously.

Wow! I think to myself, *I am an acrobat!*

Balancing myself on the ledge is getting more difficult. I slowly slide myself down from where I am perched on the ledge. *I had better not fall,* I think to myself. My feet hit the stairs again. Pausing for a second and making sure the coast is still clear, I resume my mission. I creep down the last six stairs. When my foot hits the linoleum floor, I raise my fist and whisper, *Yeah! I made it!*

The hallway to the kitchen is just as dark as my trip from the bedroom I share with my sister. I don't feel too afraid. I know making it as far as I have means I am almost there. The linoleum flooring is cold to the touch. It makes me walk faster. I hear rustling somewhere off to my left and the jingle of dog tags.

"Oh shoot!" I whisper under my breath. I had forgotten about the dogs.

My fists instinctively ball up into fists, as the dogs' growling breaks the silence. Then the dogs start barking! *BARK BARK!* I stop in my tracks. Our two dogs Mugsy and Duchess come flying out at me. I bend down to speak to them.

"Shh, shh, it's okay, it's just me."

I reach out to pet them, almost frantically because I don't want their barking to wake everyone up. Running my hands over their furry backs, they eventually quiet down. I break into a bit of a run to get to the kitchen.

Finally! Destination reached. Darkness plays tricks with my eyes. I see shadows everywhere. There's tightness in my chest. I gulp nervously and then take four deep breaths. I move forward. I see the outline of the kitchen table and chairs and the hulking refrigerator. The microwave's digital clock is blinking 3:10 a.m. "That time can't be right," I whisper to myself. "There's no way I am down here this early!"

I walk to the fridge and open it.

A blast of cold air hits me as the fridge door opens. I'm surprised the door doesn't creak. My eyes scan the four shelves laden down with food. I see various colours of cheese, a jar of dill pickles, ketchup, a package of Oscar Meyer hotdogs, and other food. I salivate as I look at the various foods before me. I know that I can only take something small though, like a roll or two, maybe a packet of Kool aid. Ah! My sister and I loved to put our fingers into the packet and then lick the powder off.

I shut the fridge door and turn to the breadbasket that sits just an arm's length away. I reach up above to try and grab the dinner rolls, but I'm too short. Grr... I eye a kitchen chair and pull it over towards the counter. I'm getting even more daring now. My desire for food is overwhelming and overriding the need to be as quiet as possible. I throw caution to the wind.

I hop onto the chair, leaning over the counter to open the cupboard door in front of me. I've seen my parents bring out peanut butter before from here. I decide that I will make peanut butter sandwiches. I find the Skippy peanut butter right away. My six-year-old hands barely reach around the whole jar and the peanut butter almost drops.

This mission is difficult! Standing on the chair, I grab two dinner rolls and quickly get off the chair and head to the cutlery drawer. After fumbling for a knife in the cutlery drawer, I find a bread-and-butter knife and crudely cut the rolls in half, before slathering a ridiculous amount of peanut butter on the rolls. Before I close the peanut butter jar, I stick the knife in one more time. Smacking my lips, I take one last taste and carefully screw the lid back onto the jar. I nimbly jump back up on the chair and put the peanut butter jar back in the cupboard. Once again, I jump down and put the chair back into its position at the table.

It's time to head back upstairs. I shove the rolls into my housecoat pocket and start walking. I don't think about the lint that will attach itself to the sandwiches I just made. Nor do I think about what may happen as I exit the kitchen and head back up the stairs.

The trip back seems to go a little faster. I feel proud of myself. I have food for my sister and me. To help navigate the stairs better, I hold my housecoat up a little. My head is down as I try to focus on getting back up the stairs and into our bedroom. I don't see the lights turn on in the bedroom to the left of the stairway or that my granny has stepped out from the spare bedroom and is standing there waiting for me to look up. When I do, I jump! I feel my heart double in speed as I'm caught in a staring war with my granny.

"Christine, what are you doing?" she asks. "Do you know what time it is? Why are you downstairs?"

I gulp nervously.

"Granny, I wasn't doing anything," I say.

Granny is standing there in the dimly lit hallway. Her short grey hair is messed up from sleep, and her eyes are squinting at me, as if she is checking that it is really me standing on the step below her.

My hands let go of my housecoat, and instinctively I stuff my hands in my pockets. My little fingers clutch the dinner rolls in my pocket. I look up at Granny.

"What's in your pockets then?" she asks.

"Nothing, nothing I swear!" I whine back.

My granny motions for me to come up the last two stairs.

"Turn your pockets out then," she says.

I head up the last two stairs and stand in front of her. I pull my pockets inside out, wishing that I could make the rolls that are in my pocket disappear. The two dinner rolls fall to the floor. My granny picks them up.

"Wait until your father finds out about this!" she says.

I start crying. My crying wakes up my parents, and my father comes out of the master bedroom. Rubbing sleep from his eyes, he squints at my granny and me.

"What is going on?"

"Christine was downstairs. I just caught her. She stole food from the fridge," granny replies.

My memory is foggy from this point on, but I do recall that I didn't sleep with my Holly Hobbie blanket or sleep in my twin bed again, after that night. Instead, as punishment, for the next month, I was made to sleep in my parent's walk-in closet with just a thin sleeping bag to cover me up. I never shared a bedroom with my sister again either.

Shortly after this mission, my granny flew back to Scotland. The spare bedroom that she had occupied became mine. I was moved into the spare bedroom. Locks, a bolt, and an alarm were soon installed on the door. There were no more whispered requests from my sister to go to the kitchen or trips to make peanut butter sandwiches in the middle of the night.

My mission failed.

MY GREAT ESCAPE

I believe I was about nine or ten years old, at the time of my great escape. I had been thinking about running away for a few days. After I woke up, once again staring at the four dull light-brown walls around me, I knew I had to go. I was tired of my situation. My bedroom consisted of a wooden bunk bed, a dresser and a desk and chair that faced a window. Sunlight might have poured in, but my curtains were often drawn. My bedroom served as my prison. It had bolts on the door. There was an alarm that would go off shrilly if I even touched the doorknob.

There was no jumping out of my bed, or feeling any excitement at the new day ahead, because to make any noise meant punishment. Punishment came in the form of a few good swats on my behind with a flyswatter, or a strike across the face with an open palm that made me cringe inside and want to cry. Crying was not allowed because my adoptive parents were quick to anger. Though I never knew what punishment may come, the worst was always being locked up, and sometimes one of them coming into my room sent my heart into my throat. I always felt like a mere glance would make them go off. Crying was best done in private when I thought there was no one around to hear me.

As soon as I heard footsteps outside my bedroom door, my little body would tense up and my heart would speed up. I never knew what would greet me, a sarcastic smile or a withering glare for some imagined sin that would make me the target of another torrent of angry words or a beating.

That day I was tired. Tired of being held hostage—I wanted to be free. But first, I was served breakfast. I remember clearly, the sound of the bolts on my door being undone, the sharp ping as the alarm was shut off. The door opened and there was my adoptive father with a tray in his hands. My breakfast lay upon it.

Breakfast for me consisted of two slices of white bread with peanut butter and jelly spread thinly upon them, cut into four little perfect squares. The tray was put down onto my desk, I was told to eat, and my adoptive father exited. I did not leave the edge of my bed until he had left the room, and I heard the locks going back into place, and the alarm being turned back on. I ran over to my desk, as soon as I heard my father's footsteps disappear down the hall. I looked at my food, sat at my desk and hungrily gulped the sandwich down. My stomach grumbled but not in hunger, it grumbled with anxiety and a fear that my nine or ten-year-old mind could not figure out.

As I ate, I was careful to not make a mess of any kind. I was trained and trained well. I learned to be as quiet as possible, to not make any messes and to only do what I had to do when I was given the okay. Just like a puppy obeying his master.

I recall eating my sandwich, rearranging everything on my tray, making sure that everything was lined up perfectly, getting up from my desk and tiptoeing to my bedroom door to knock and let someone, anyone know, I had to go to the washroom. The bathroom was across the hall from my bedroom. It felt like an eternity before my door was finally opened and I was marched across the hall to do my deed, and then marched back to my room. The door would be closed and locked behind me once more.

My adoptive mother was a stay-at-home mom. She did not have to work because our adoptive father was the breadwinner in the family. But for some reason that day, everyone left the house early. My sister and I were left behind. I did not know where my older brothers were and I really did not care, because they never paid any attention to me anyways. I listened anxiously as I heard the hustle and bustle of everyone getting ready to leave. I didn't know where anyone was going, but after hearing the front door close, there was a weird kind of silence that settled around the house and filtered up to my bedroom. I knew that the silence meant I could relax and let my guard down.

Playing in my room was boring. I could only play so long with my Barbie dolls, dressing them up and pretending they were my friends or that I was their mom and taking care of them, as I carefully brushed their hair and spoke to them. They were my only company in that bedroom. I remember having some paper, and a short stubby little pencil. My sister could have given it to me, my memory is not too clear here, but sometimes I would pass the time with drawing.

Sometimes I would sit cross-legged at my desk or I would lie on my stomach on the floor and draw whatever came to my mind. I shared my drawings and/or scribblings with my sister because sometimes when no one was around, she would come and sit outside my bedroom door. She would whisper "Hey Christine," and I would go and sit by the door on my side. If she told me no one was there, I would pass my scribblings to her by putting them under my door for her to grab. My sister was ten months older, my friend, and my ally. She would look at my drawings or my scribblings from the other side of the door. I distinctly remember her telling me, "Good job!"

I yearned to hear kind words, to hear appreciation of some kind, and my sister would do that when we had those rare moments of keeping each other company through my closed door. When my sister sat outside my bedroom door, we would talk about anything that came to mind. That day, I whispered to her through the locked bedroom door, that I wanted to run away. I wanted to be free.

My sister and I were allies in the situation we lived in and I know she must have pondered how I was feeling, and known that by letting me go free, even if it was only for an hour or so, I would feel happy. I do not think she really thought of what could happen to her, let alone me, by unlocking my door and letting me go. I remember hearing her go down the hallway, and then hearing the dragging of a chair so that she could reach the bolts on my door and unlock them. I remember my elation when I heard my bedroom door become unlocked, heard the ping as the alarm was turned off, and the door was opened. I was *FREE!*

At first, I was afraid to come out of my room. I briefly wondered if the door being open was real, or if it was a trick meant to cause me to get another beating. My eyes were wide like a little deer's frozen in headlights. I didn't know what to do or what to say. But then I smiled at my sister, the biggest smile I could muster up from inside, and I sprang into action.

I was free! At the time it meant more to me than the fear of what could happen to me or to my sister if our parents found out. I remember leaving that big house where our neighbours thought our family lived the perfect life. I had my coat on, and I carried a backpack, with a couple of books. After all, I could not leave those behind! I had a loaf of bread and twenty dollars that my sister had carefully taken from our oldest brother's room.

"The loaf of bread is for when you get hungry," my sister told me.

I recall my little legs pumping as I ran out the front door of the house, and my heart pounding as I got to the street. I looked both ways as I left the front yard and walked along as nonchalantly as I could.

"Don't look suspicious," I kept telling myself.

I knew that I had to be careful about my parents seeing me, so every once in a while as I walked, I would see a bush, hide behind it, pop out from behind it, run for a little bit, stop and then hide once more.

The first stop in my great escape was at a convenience store. I walked into the store and went around looking at everything. As I was wandering, I noticed that the store clerk was looking at me kind of funny, so I grabbed a brown bag from the counter. The bag was the size of a lunch bag. I went to the candy section and began to fill my bag with everything that I could possibly think of. Oh, the days of five cent candies and penny gum! After I filled my bag, I went to the counter, reached up and gave my twenty dollars to the clerk. In my nine- to ten-year-old mind, I did not see anything wrong with buying a huge bag of candy. I was in heaven!

I left the convenience store and carried on with my journey. By that time, I had walked across six big blocks. It was a feat that I felt proud of. Somehow, I made it to my friend's house. Here it was, bright and early, and I was standing below her bedroom window. Knowing that I could not yell, I picked up a few pebbles, and threw them at her window. My friend's name was Natalie. She poked her head out her window.

"What are you doing?" she asked me. "My mom is going to hear you!"

But I did not care.

"I am free," I told her. "I ran away, and I am never going back."

I fantasized that I could go and live with my friend Natalie and her family, and my adoptive parents would never have to see me again. But that thought was quickly squashed, when out of the corner of my eye I saw my friend's mom come around the corner in her pajamas.

"What are you doing, Christine?" she asked me.

My resolve broke down and I burst into tears. Through my tears I told her that I had run away, that my parents would not miss me, and that I wanted to live with them because I did not ever want to go back to my adoptive parents and their house again.

The enormity of my situation hit me. I realized I had put my friend's family in an awkward situation because I had blatantly told them that I had run away and they would have to call the police. I was more afraid than I was letting on.

My friend's mom walked to where I was standing below her daughter's window, gently pulled me into her arms, hugged me, and said, "Come on, Christine. Let's go inside." With her arm around me, she gently steered me into their house. I remember entering their house, taking my shoes off, and sitting in their living room. As I looked around anxiously, my friend came out of her bedroom in her nightgown.

"Hi, Christine," she said rather quietly.

Natalie's mom let her daughter take me to her bedroom for a few minutes. We sat quietly in her room and then we were called for breakfast. I gobbled my food down as though I had not eaten in weeks. In the background, I felt the eyes of Natalie's parents on me. They briefly left the kitchen while Natalie and I had breakfast and went into the next room. I heard them whispering and saying,

"We have to call someone," they whispered. "We have to do something—she can't stay here, with no one knowing."

I was happy I was at my friend's house, but as I sat at my friend's kitchen table, I heard the phone being picked up, and the rotary dial making a swooshing noise as each number was dialed. A few minutes passed then her parents came back into the room. "You'll have to go back home," they told me. "But we'll take you to school first. Your parents will pick you up there."

After my friend got herself ready, we all put our coats on, and left the house. My friend's mom drove us to the school in a mere five minutes. I was guided into the secretary's office. My friend's mom was ushered into the adjoining room, the principal's office. As she quietly spoke to the principal, my heart grew heavy.

The principal called my mother, and after what seemed like an eternity, she showed up at the school. I knew she was angry, and more than likely embarrassed. Her face was red, and she stood in front of the principal and I in a stance that meant I was in big trouble. I stood there and tried to put the most defiant look on my face. To keep up appearances, my mother apologized to my friend's mom for my unexpected visit. The Scottish lilt in her voice was a bit more palpable than usual. She grabbed me by the shoulder, and I could feel her nails digging into my shoulder. I went home with her rather grudgingly.

Years later, I found out that when my parents discovered I wasn't in my room, they grilled my sister. My sister would not admit to unlocking my door. She let them believe that I had somehow managed to open my bedroom window, climb out the window; slide down from the roof and onto the sidewalk. I call it my great escape because for the longest time my parents never understood how I got out of my room. When I look back on it now, it makes me laugh. I realize now that the bond my sister and I had while we lived in that situation was what got me through the roughest moments. We had each other's backs and taught each other courage, and that was something we both needed in order to survive.

Not long after this incident, I was informed that I would be going to a boarding school. My things were packed, and I was dropped off at a home called Maryvale, a group home for troubled kids.

MARYVALE

The group home I was sent to was on the other side of Windsor which was far from where I had been raised—the south side. The homes were not as big, there were a lot more industrial buildings, and Maryvale was tucked away from everyone and everything, like the kids who stayed there didn't matter. I didn't get many visitors; actually none, unless it was a staff member from another cottage coming to get me to take me to the activities building across the way from the cottage I lived in.

I remember the little cottages of my group home. I lived in Cottage #3. It was a three-floor spread on a tract of land owned by the Five Sisters of the Roman Catholic Order of the Good Shepherd. I knew the floors of the cottage intimately. I would pace the floors back and forth inside my room, run down the hallway when a staff member called my name, and when doing one of my chores, I'd swish the mop from one end of the hallway to the other. I shared a bedroom with another girl. My bed consisted of a thin mattress on a metal frame, with sheets and blankets folded on it in military style. There was nothing homey about it. It wasn't like the bedroom that I had had at my adoptive parents'. There I had bunk beds, and could choose the bottom bunk or the top bunk, even though I was the only one occupying the bedroom. I had a small pile of Barbies that I could play with, and scraps of paper I could draw or write on while I wondered when I would be let out of my bedroom next.

I spent a lot of time in my bedroom at Cottage #3, not because I was made to, but because I was the youngest of all the girls who lived there. I was ten years old, and they were fourteen years old and higher. I couldn't really relate to anyone, and preferred to spend my time alone. After all, I had grown used to it when I was living with my adoptive family since they kept me apart from everyone in the house, locked away in my bedroom.

My adoptive father and my sister came to visit me at Maryvale for about a month, and then, without warning, the visits ceased. It was devastating for me. It not only meant that I was without parents, but that I was away from my biological sister. I was put back in the care of the Children's Aid Society, and once again, was a part of the child welfare system. Not long afterwards, I was made a Crown Ward.

I remember lying on my bed in this strange new building, hugging a little pink brocaded pillow I'd had since I was in kindergarten. I often found myself hugging that pillow. On it was a little white label with my name written in pen. Tears silently falling, I would hold the pillow and stare out the window, wondering what was so bad about me, that my parents didn't want me.

I grew up quickly in this group home. I learned things before I should have. I remember how I entered the shared bathroom and saw one of the girls with a razor shaving her legs, and the trickle of blood that showed on her skin, as she pulled the razor up and down, up and down.

"What are you doing?" I asked her. "Can I do that too?"

"Sure, you can shave too, if you want Christine."

"What else do you shave besides your legs?" I asked her.

The girl grinned. "You shave your arms too," she said.

In my naivety, I didn't realize that the girl meant you shave your armpits, and because I wanted to be cool like her, I later found a razor and shaved all the hair off my forearms. I ran out of the bathroom fifteen minutes later.

"I'm a big girl now," I told a staff member standing at the door of their office "because I shaved."

I didn't see the cuts on my arms from the razor or feel the trickle of blood that welled up on the cuts. It wasn't that bad, but I remember one of the staff leading me to a chair and having me sit with her, while she explained what shaving meant, and how I was too young to do that yet.

As I became accustomed to living at Maryvale, I often found myself wanting to spend time with a few of the staff members. In turn, those staff members at my cottage tried to keep me happy and occupied. They would give me hugs and take me for walks around the group home and the grounds. Sometimes when everyone else was away visiting with their families they took me to their homes for a holiday.

When I misbehaved at Maryvale, I had to spend time in the quiet room. No one received special treatment when they misbehaved, and so everyone dreaded the quiet room. Oh, how I remember that quiet room. The thin little mattress that was laid out in the middle of the floor, the flimsy blanket that never kept you warm enough, the door that was locked behind you, and the loneliness that crept over you as you sat there all alone. Depending on your crime (mouthing back to staff, losing your temper, or running away), you could be there for up to seventy-two hours. How long you stayed in the quiet room was left to the staff's discretion.

Then one day I found out I could no longer contact my sister. I was sitting in the telephone room which was located off the dining room. I was excited because I was going to be calling my sister. I usually called her every Sunday. I remember my little fingers dialing the number. My heart was pounding as I recall hearing the operator coming onto the phone and the words 'this number is no longer in service.' I thought that I had made a mistake. I hung up the phone and dialed again. I heard the same message. My world changed in a matter of seconds.

I slammed the phone down so hard that the receiver fell off the cradle, and the phone tipped over and hit the floor. I tried to pick up the phone and put it back on the table. Anger and fear began coursing through me, but, at the time, I could not articulate how I felt. I started to scream and swear randomly using the few choice words I had heard from the other residents in my cottage. "Oh shit!" "Fuck!"

At ten years old, those words were fairly new to me. People think that at ten years old, you know a few swear words, but I really didn't learn any until I reached Maryvale and heard the words from other residents. I thought, if they can swear, I can swear too! As I was swearing and banging things around, the staff came running from the office on the third floor. One staff member stood at the top of the stairs, while another grabbed me. I remember Bob's arms wrapping around me and feeling trapped. I couldn't run. I was kicking and screaming and crying all at once. Bob tried to tell me to calm down, but I couldn't. In the distance I heard the other staff member at the top of the stairs say, "take her downstairs."

To the dungeon I went.

With his arms wrapped around me, Bob carried me from the brightly lit foyer of the cottage into the dark basement. I counted the doorways as we went down the hallway, hearing his footsteps as we went. 1… 2… 3… 4… "I promise, I promise I'll be good," I stuttered as the tears fell, and my head began to pound.

"I don't want to be down here!" I screamed.

Bob acted like he hadn't heard me and strode purposefully down the hall. He stopped at door number 4, the room farthest from the stairwell, where no one can hear you yell, no matter how loud you are.

The rest of that day was a blur. After the door closed behind me in the quiet room, I just laid on the mattress that was provided for me, with my knees pulled closely to my chest, and my arms wrapped around them. I wanted a hug, someone to comfort me, to tell me that I would be okay, instead I was alone, and I cried until I nodded off to sleep.

I slept rather fitfully on that thin little mattress. I had nothing to do in that room. I lay there, my mind racing a mile a minute. Tears flowed regularly. While I was there, various staff members came in and out with a tray of food. Every time they came in I asked, "When can I get out of here?" and their reply was always, "As soon as you can behave."

I don't recall how long I stayed in the quiet room, but I learned that as long as I stayed quiet and didn't yell or bang on the door, my time in the quiet room lessened. Finally, I heard the door being unlocked.

"You can come out, Christine," a staff member said.

I jumped from the mattress on the floor and bolted out the door as if a fire had been lit behind me. The staff member followed close behind.

Shortly after my stint in the quiet room, my life started to rapidly change. I was no longer an innocent little girl waiting to go home to her parents. I was an orphan. Word of my new status spread around my cottage. Soon everyone knew about my adoptive parents giving me up. Hushed whispers greeted me when I turned a corner or entered a room. Some staff members would look at me and I knew they felt sorry for me because they would give me a big hug even though they had never hugged me before. They were the kind of hugs that made me want to cling to the person giving them to me and say, "Don't leave me too!"

YOU ARE NOT WANTED

I'm sitting at a long brown table; a table scratched and worn by God knows how many people who sat here before me. My feet barely touch the ground. An older lady sits beside me. She leans over and whispers to me.

"I am your lawyer. My name is Helen Carefoot."

I look at her as if to say, "I really don't care."

Deep down I am frightened. My heart is thumping, and I silently nod my head. Before me, I see a huge expanse of brown-carpeted floor, and a large desk where the judge is sitting. Near the judge are two sitting areas—I later find out one is where the court clerk sits to type up her notes and the other is where the plaintiff or defendant sits to tell their story. I glance up briefly to see my adoptive father stride across the floor and raise his hand. He tells the court clerk: "I swear to tell the truth and nothing but the truth."

He looks ahead, careful not to look over to where I am sitting. He treats me like a stranger and then sits down at the court officer's request.

The fear inside me starts to consume me. I want to be sick. My heart goes into my throat. I take a huge gulp. I will my heart to slow down. I tell myself *"I can't cry. I need to be brave."*

I don't want to show my adoptive parents that what they're doing is ripping my heart out. I don't want them to know they're leaving me so scared and vulnerable.

I don't know how long I sat there.

******

For a ten-year-old, court is pretty boring. Everything that was being said went over my head. I sat at the table with a piece of paper and pencil before me, in case I wanted to doodle. I don't really remember hearing what was said. I do know that I did come alive when I heard the judge say, "Sir, you need to speak louder!"

When I heard the judge say that I bit my lip to stop myself from laughing out loud. I smiled and thought, *it's about time that someone yelled at him!* I abruptly stopped smiling when I heard my adoptive father speak.

"Christine is not wanted," he said. "We give her up to the care of the Children's Aid Society."

After I heard those words, things became a blur. I do remember the court session ending and walking out of the courtroom to the elevator. My lawyer was with me. We were both quiet. I wanted to cry but I couldn't. I kept it inside. My head was spinning, my little fists clenched at my sides. My insides were in turmoil. Despite their violence and abuse, it was terrifying to know I didn't have parents anymore. I was an orphan.

When I was in the elevator about to leave the courthouse, my adoptive mother said, "see ya!" She said it out of habit, but this time it felt ominous. I wanted to cry even more because I knew I wouldn't be seeing her again.

The enormity of what had happened in the courtroom didn't hit me until much later. I didn't realize at the time that this would probably be the last time I would see my adoptive parents. Years later I would find out that, after that court room appearance, my adoptive mother considered me dead to her. The anger and hurt that would consume me from that point on was because I was torn away from everything I had known.

On some level, I did know that my adoptive parents were going to give me up because I had been missing school over and over again just to go to court. Classmates were quiet around me when I was in class, and it wasn't until months later that I learned my grade six teacher had told the class while I was away at one point that "Christine needs to be kept in our prayers." I knew she meant well but I felt so invaded because then everyone in my class knew I had no parents.

After the court had made their decision, and I was taken back to Maryvale, I began to close myself off from those around me. It was the only way I knew to keep myself safe because I did not want to go through such pain again. The pain didn't go away though, it festered inside me more, especially upon my return to Maryvale.

Knowing that I no longer had parents and that I might not see my sister again, the anger inside me grew and I ran away every chance I got. I didn't care that I would get caught and taken back to Maryvale to face more punishment for running away.

While lying in the time out room after my escapes, I had nothing to look at but the bare walls. I had no contact with anyone, unless it was a staff member bringing me a meal. This was reminiscent of what my adoptive parents had been doing to me for a year before I landed in the care of Maryvale. The mattress I laid on was thin and lumpy, the blanket that was given to me barely kept me warm, but I told myself I didn't really care.

I thought about how a month before I was given up I had been sitting in my grade five class. I excitedly told a few kids that I was going to a boarding school and I would be moving. The thought that I was going to a boarding school was something that seemed exotic. It was something that in my ten-year-old mind I thought only the rich did. I didn't realize that I was heading to a place where other kids and I were essentially cast aside.

Being given up was something I felt immense shame about. When I was fourteen years old, my sister had somehow located where I was living, and had begun to call me. I didn't know until years later that my adoptive father had somehow been keeping track of everywhere I was placed. He eventually arranged for me to visit my sister. Our reunion took place at a local mall in my former hometown.

I don't recall this visit that well. I felt a lot of trepidation when I saw my adoptive father standing there inside the entrance of the mall with my sister standing beside him. He told my sister, "You have an hour to visit and then we must head back home."

The visit was brief, and I didn't see my biological sister again until I was seventeen. My experiences of being given up by my adoptive parents, not seeing my sister, and being in the care of the Children's Aid and the child welfare system, made me wise beyond my years, yet I was still a little girl at heart. I was a little girl who wanted love and acceptance and didn't care if she died in the process.

Throughout the years I was separated from my sister, I missed her immensely. I often wondered how she was doing, and worried that she had become the subject of the abuse I had experienced. If she did experience the same abuse, how could she deal with it? Because we were separated neither of us could protect the other anymore. Each of us was alone.

I am an adult now and far away from those who hurt me. I rebuilt my life and I have surrounded myself with people who believe in me and encourage me to not only keep up the fight but to stay strong. Today, I am alive, and I am strong because I am a survivor. I am a survivor in a sea of thousands of other First Nations children who were forced into the child welfare system through no fault of their own. I know that I am not alone.

Grade one.

THE DESK

After being at Maryvale for a year, a couple who worked at Maryvale decided to take me in. Their names were Bob and Tracey, and they had a one-year-old son, Lucas. I was eleven years old when I moved into this, my first foster home. Not long after I moved to Bob and Tracey's house, they gave me a welcome gift: a beautiful wooden desk. The desk was solid wood with a little ink well on the top left side. Every day, I lovingly organized my pens and pencils and the notebooks I kept inside. It was the first thing I had ever really owned, and I loved that I had been given such a beautiful gift. I spent a lot of time hunched over my desk, writing or drawing. I felt such pride having something I could call my own.

I sat at the desk day in and day out, daydreaming as I looked out my bedroom window, taking in the flowering of the trees, or watching a car slowly go by. I did my homework and coloured at this desk. I even sat there when my social worker from the Children's Aid Society visited. She would sit at the edge of my bed while I sat at my desk telling her what I had been doing since the last time I had seen her.

One day, I decided to etch my name into the surface of the desk. There was something so satisfying about seeing my name— CHRISTINE—carved into the desk. It made me feel proud and told the world that this desk was mine!

One particular day, I was argumentative with my foster parents, and as a consequence, my foster mom had come in to try to speak with me. As usual, I was sitting at my desk. She came right up beside me and as she was trying to reason with me, she looked down and noticed that I had etched my name into the surface of the top of the desk.

I remember her face turning red.

"When the hell did you do that?" she yelled. "Why? Why would you do that?"

My heart leapt into my throat, and I shrugged my shoulders. I didn't know why I had done it; I had just done it on a whim. That day, because I couldn't explain my actions, my foster mom told me, "We will never give you something like this again."

The consequences that followed began a downhill journey for my time at this foster home. First, my desk was removed from my room, Later that night, my foster dad marched into my room and took the desk, much to my dismay.

"Where are you going with my desk?" I asked. "That's my desk, you can't take it."

"If you're going to deface property, this desk is no longer yours to keep."

I had thought that because the desk had been given to me, that it was mine to keep. I didn't realize that items given to me could be so easily taken away.

"I hate you!" I yelled as he left my room. I slammed my bedroom door and threw myself onto my bed, crying uncontrollably. I was crying more out of anger than anything else. After about an hour of being on my own, I was called out of my room. My foster dad, though calm in his anger, was stern.

"You will refinish this desk," he said. "That means sanding it, staining it, and bringing it back to what it looked like when we first gave it to you."

I hung my head and said, "Okay."

The desk was put in the basement of my foster home. Every day after school and on weekends, I had to go to the basement. With the sandpaper clenched in my fist, I scrubbed and scrubbed at the desk for what seemed like hours. As an eleven-year-old, I despised this work. I wanted to be outside riding my bike or anywhere but stuck in a basement sanding a desk. In retrospect, I realize I had brought it on myself.

While working in the basement, an allergy to dust began to affect me. I started sneezing repeatedly and getting nosebleeds. The nosebleeds happened so often that my foster parents thought I was playing a trick to get myself out of working on the desk. In frustration, they once again moved my desk, and this time put it outside underneath their carport. The desk was flimsily protected from the outdoor elements by the carport's roof and was sandwiched between a car and a wire fence that led to their backyard.

Each day I was told to "get to work." I remember standing under the carport, feeling the roughness of the sandpaper in my hand and the contempt I felt for them for making me do this work. I stood outside with a piece of sandpaper clenched in my fist. My shoulders were tense, and my back was aching as I ran the sandpaper back and forth, back and forth. The dust occasionally made me sneeze and my nose would become congested. I didn't have any Kleenex, so I would sniff and hope I wouldn't get another nosebleed.

I had been working on my desk for days; and the sanding was not getting me anywhere. I don't know how long I was outside on this particular day. It felt like forever, "I'm not going to take anymore crap," I told myself. "And I am not going to keep sanding this desk if it means that I can't ride my bike or play." My play time had been taken away just because I had carved my name into my desk. Enough is enough, I decided.

All of a sudden, the stillness around me was broken by the sound of the backdoor of the house opening. My foster dad materialized with his son Lucas by his side.

"We have to go get groceries. You stay here and continue working," he said. He put Lucas into his car seat, got into the car, and slammed the car door.

As the car left the driveway and turned the corner, I impulsively decided to make my move. I stopped sanding, stretched, and put the sandpaper down. I walked to the end of the driveway, looked both ways and began walking. The tension in my shoulders dissipated. I was not afraid; I just walked.

I walked aimlessly and for quite some time. I must have lost track of time because one minute I was in suburbia, and before I realized it, I was in the middle of nowhere, walking on the side of a wide paved street called Malden Road. The houses were spaced far apart, and the only noise I could hear was cars whizzing by, as I carefully tried to stay as far away from the cars as I could.

I stopped on a stretch of Malden Road, trying to figure out where I was heading. I had never had a good sense of direction, so being lost had me feeling scared and confused. I must have looked more scared than I thought because out of the blue, when I looked up, I saw a stranger walking slowly towards me.

"Are you ok?" she asked. "Where are you heading?"

I looked over at her and blurted out, "I ran away."

A look of shock overtook the lady's face, but calmly, she told me, "Well, come with me, and my husband and I can get you some help."

At first, I was a little reluctant to go with her, but for some reason with this stranger, I felt safe. She took my hand and guided me towards her house. We walked across an expanse of bright green grass, and up a little sidewalk. We entered her house and she had me sit at her kitchen table. I could smell the dinner she had been cooking for her family. My stomach was rumbling, as she walked over to her refrigerator, and asked me, "Would you like some milk?"

"Yes, I would," I said and gulped the milk down in a matter of seconds after she handed me a glass.

Though I don't recall her name, this woman made me feel comfortable, but I knew I wasn't going to be able to stay there forever. Her husband and two kids came into the house and sat at the kitchen table with me. I remember eating corn on the cob, and the whispering between the couple as they tried to figure out who to call without getting me riled up.

Eventually, they called the police. I heard them speaking to them on the phone. I ran from their kitchen into their living room and hid in the corner beside a big plant.

"We can't keep you," they kept telling me. "You have to go back home."

I began crying.

"I don't wanna go home. I'm not going to go with the police when they come here," I told them petulantly.

It wasn't long until the doorbell rang, and I heard the man say, "Hello Officer, thank you for coming."

The officer came into the living room to try to get me to go with him and his partner. He was a well-built muscular man with a buzz cut. At first, he took his cap off and held it in front of himself while he tried to coax me out of the corner. He was the good cop; his partner played the bad cop. We all know how that goes.

"Hey, you're just a little baby aren't you?" his partner said.

I adamantly told him, "I am not a baby!" but he kept goading me on. After about fifteen minutes of goading me, he strode over to where I was standing, reached out and lifted me right off the ground. With his arms wrapped around me I couldn't make any moves.

"We have to take you back home. You're coming with us, whether you want to or not," he said.

The officer carried me out to their police cruiser, and in the split second he loosened his grip to open the cruiser door, I hauled off and kicked him in the shin. He put me down abruptly at the back door of their cruiser, put his hand on my head, and pushed my head down, telling me, "get in the car." I knew he was angry, and I had no room to get past him to try to run again, so I complied.

As I sat in the back of the police cruiser, I heard the two officers thank the lady and her husband for looking out for me. A few days (or maybe it was weeks) after being returned to my foster home by the police, I was sent to summer camp and told I would return in two weeks. During those two weeks, a camp counsellor pulled me aside.

"You won't be going back to your foster home," the counsellor said. "You'll be going somewhere else."

I never went back to that foster home, and I never saw my desk again. Years later, I called them and set up a visit. It took a number of phone calls and chats on the phone before they trusted me enough to grant me a visit. The visit was awkward and held at a restaurant they chose. Both of them have since passed. I learned that the foster mom had committed suicide, and the foster dad had passed as a result of complications from heart surgery.

After graduating from high school.

BURNING QUESTIONS

I had teenage angst just like any other teenager, but the angst I felt inside was something I felt no one around me could understand. It was while I was in my third foster home that the emptiness I felt inside began to fester and grow bigger than me. I couldn't quite explain this emptiness and it gnawed at me continuously. I often wondered, *will this emptiness ever go away or will it slowly kill me?*

As a teenager, I lived in a small town called Kingsville, where I stood out—a brown face in a sea of white faces. I had transferred from my second foster home in Windsor to a small town where, more than anything, I felt alone. The transfer happened in the middle of my grade eight year. I remember thinking: What a time to transfer!

In the small town there was racism that was not always noticeable to those around me, but I experienced it. The racism was subtle but it was there. It was there when I was the last one picked for team sports at school. It was there when no one sat with me at lunch time, and the only person who would talk with me was my teacher. Because no one in my age group would talk to me, I would hang out with younger students. I found they were less discriminating and more accepting of who I was. I would get teased for that, so at recess I walked with the teacher on yard duty instead of socializing with the other kids my age. I would walk in companionable silence with whatever teacher was on yard duty and I felt safe. I sought attention from the school principal by telling him I was sick and needed to go home. He was a short, balding man, but he would put his arm around me, smile and say, "Christine, it's ok, you're okay."

But those words couldn't cure a lonely heart or the emptiness I felt. I would start to cry and tell him, "I can't stay; I want to go home!" I'm sure my foster mom at the time didn't know the real reason why I wanted to be at home instead of school. She never asked me why. She just accepted that I wanted to be at home. She would give permission for me to come back home for the day, as long as I promised that I would go back to school the next day.

Don't get me wrong here, I excelled at school, but I always knew that I was the different one everywhere I went. I would go to bed at night and in the deep recesses of my mind I would ask myself repeatedly, "I wonder if my mom is alive? Will I ever find her? What does she look like? Will she want to see me?" I kept these questions to myself because I really didn't know who I could talk to about them. The questions nagged at me constantly and heightened my feelings of not knowing who I was, where I would fit in, or if I would ever find the family I longed for so deeply.

HIGH SCHOOL YEARS

My high school years were a blur. The angst inside me grew in leaps and bounds, and I dealt with it by not only continuing to limit my food intake, but also becoming a perfectionist. I pushed myself to obtain high marks and studied like crazy. I also became what I later understood to be obsessive compulsive. I had to have everything in order and lined up. Every month I rearranged everything in the bedroom I had in my foster home and while doing that, I cleaned the walls with a cleaner and a scrub brush, washing them from top to bottom.

I think the chores that my foster mom gave me fed into my OCD even more. Every weekend, I had to do the dusting in the TV room. Because there were a lot of knick-knacks, I had to methodically go over everything with a cloth, and make sure that there was no dust on anything when I finished. My foster mom would inspect my dusting and there were a number of times that I would have to restart my dusting because she would see a speck of dust.

These foster parents, Lois and Gary, were strict, and though I despised it at the time, after I left their home, I realized why their strictness was needed. It gave me discipline, and provided a type of structure for me. Structure had been lacking in my life. But the structure that was provided developed into my obsessive compulsiveness, and learning how to control it was another battle that I fought daily, albeit silently.

I had a few friends in high school, but there were only one or two whom I would invite over. The other friends I just hung around with in between classes or after school for a few minutes. There was one friend in particular who I really enjoyed spending time with. That was Jodie, who became my best friend. She was a quiet girl, with long curly hair, and a slim build. Though she learned a lot about my background during our conversations, she never made me feel out of place, or questioned who I was. Jodie and I would hang out in my bedroom, listening to music and chatting. Jodie introduced me to various types of music. We loved hard rock, and we would blare the likes of Guns and Roses, Def Leppard, and Bon Jovi.

Blaring my music sometimes got me in trouble. Lois and Gary installed an intercom in my room, and if I was playing my music too loud, one of their voices would come over the intercom telling me to turn it off.

When I got my first cassette tape of Bon Jovi for Christmas, I was super excited. I played the tape in my cassette player until the tape literally broke. I also began to listen to pop music and what my friends would call sappy music—Air Supply, Jennifer Warnes, and Bette Midler.

I have always loved music, and in high school I began to develop a deeper appreciation for it. I always wanted to know the lyrics to my favourite songs and after getting to know them, I would apply the meanings to what I was going through at the time. Music became a way for me to convey how I was feeling. When Jodie would come over, if I was playing Air Supply, she came to understand that there was something that was making me feel unhappy or really sad.

It was during this time that I saw my first CD and the recollection of that makes me laugh. Jodie had called me and had asked if I wanted to come over. She said she had something to show me.

"Ok, I'm coming right over," I said and quickly got ready.

Walking to her place only took me ten to fifteen minutes. The suburb I lived in was small but I liked looking around when I walked down Main Street in Kingsville. There were a lot of interesting mom-and-pop stores. But this time, I ignored them and rushed to Jodie's place. When I got there, she opened the door and said "My stepdad got a CD player. Do you want to listen to some music on it?"

"Sure," I said, but until then I hadn't even heard of CDs or a CD player.

After I took off my coat, and put it on Jodie's bed, we traipsed into the living room. We stopped where the CD player was, and Jodie started telling me how to use it and then took out a CD that she wanted to play. She handed it to me because I told her I wanted to take a look at it. It was a small and shiny circular disc. I blurted out, "Oh my God, these look just like little records!"

I didn't realize that her stepdad was in the front room. He came and stood under the archway to their living room and started chuckling. Then Jodie started laughing too. At first, I didn't understand why they were laughing, but then I realized that I sounded like I had just come out of the stone age and laughed with them.

Spending time with my friends was great, but I was still trying to deal with a lot of my inner pain. I always felt different not just because I was First Nations, but because everyone I spent time with had a real mom, dad, and siblings and sometimes at school there were homework assignments that explored family. I couldn't call my foster parents my real parents because they were my foster parents and not my adoptive parents, or my birth parents.

In one of my classes, we were told that our assignment was to make a family tree. I wanted to disappear into the classroom floor. There was no way I could make a family tree. Other than the biological sister whom I had been separated from, I didn't even know who my real family was at that time. I recall being excused from the assignment, which singled me out even more, but I don't remember what the teacher had me do instead.

My eating disorder, which had started when I was twelve years old, was a huge part of who I was in high school. I would walk up a flight of stairs to get to my English class, and I would hear the whispers of some of the students, "oh, that girl is anorexic, look at her." I did nothing to dissuade the comments, even though outside of school, my foster parents had me see my social worker and a family doctor to find out what they could do to help me. My foster parents didn't know what to make of my desire to not eat. But I know they tried to understand.

It got to the point that, one time, I passed out in gym class while exercising and I had to sit out that class for the rest of the period. My foster parents were called and I was sent home for the day. Lunchtimes in the cafeteria became difficult because the principal of the high school would come up to me and say, "Christine, would you like an orange?" I'd say, "Sure," and I would go as far as peeling it while he was standing there watching me over his shoulder, but the orange would never pass my lips. I would grab a napkin when I thought no one was looking and quietly fold the pieces of orange into it. It would be tossed into the garbage along with my other food.

When my foster parents called my social worker she would say, "Oh, she's doing it for attention." I was so angry at her for saying that because inside my feelings were boiling up inside me and I felt I couldn't talk about them to anyone. When I was made to see the town's doctor, he was more interested in telling me to practice safe sex than in figuring out why I was refusing to eat. Sure, he had me write down what I was eating, but I was defiant and would lie about what I had eaten. When I knew he was going to be weighing me, I would gulp down glasses of water beforehand so that my true weight wouldn't show. I had become my own worst enemy.

When I graduated from high school, I experienced new freedoms I had not known before. I had been accepted back in my hometown of Windsor at the local college for the Journalism-Print program. As part of my freedom, and despite the outcry of my foster parents, I tried to re-ignite my failed relationship with my adoptive father. He was the first one to reach out to me. I recall getting a phone call out of the blue and my foster mom Lois calling me into the kitchen where the phone was.

At first, the phone calls were pretty awkward, and a bit concerning as I had not had any contact with him until I was officially leaving my foster home for college. I don't really recall what was said in the calls, but they often consisted of him doing most of the talking and me standing with the phone in my hand and listening. Lois and Gary were concerned enough that they called my social worker Lynn from the Children's Aid Society. I think their concern made me want to rebel a bit more.

I do remember one call that I initiated. I was alone in the house and I seized that time to call. Dialing that phone and hearing his second wife's voice excitedly say, "Your father is not here at the moment, but I'll tell him you called," made my heart leap into my throat. I quickly hung up the phone, as though it was scalding hot and was burning my hand.

After that initial call, I started receiving letters from my adoptive father, and each time I got one, I opened it with trepidation. He would say things like "I didn't know what was going on, it wasn't my fault." Or he would put all the blame onto his ex-wife Janet. At first I wanted to believe him, but Lois and Gary and my social worker Lynn told me that was how he was trying to manipulate me, so that I would continue contact with him. I thought that having my adoptive father back in my life would somehow solve the angst I felt. It didn't; it deepened it. The trauma of the abuse I had gone through with them came flooding back. I remembered the physical and emotional abuse differently. I recalled the times my adoptive father put me over his knees and hit me with a flyswatter or with his bare hands. I remembered being locked up in my room, with the bolts and alarm on my door, and him guarding me at the bathroom door. I remember the time I was made to sleep in his and Janet's walk-in closet and being yelled at when I tried to crawl out to get to the bathroom

For some reason, I tried to push all of those memories aside, and in between the phone calls, a flurry of letters addressed to me would come to Lois and Gary's home. With the arrival of each letter, my foster parents noticed me withdraw inside myself even more.

When I was accepted to college in Windsor, I was also accepted at an Independent Living Home for teenagers transitioning out of care. I remember my first day at the home. My social worker Lynn had driven me from Kingsville and into Windsor right to the driveway of the Independent Living Home. I remember the key she had to the home making a clicking noise as the tumbler unlocked and the door swung open.

On the floor sat an envelope. It was a letter addressed to me. Lynn picked it up, and in disgust said, "oh, it's from your adoptive father." Lynn never approved of the letters I received from my adoptive father and she had often made it clear that my adoptive father's motive for getting back in touch with me was self-serving of him, that he was trying to put me back into a place of danger, mentally and physically.

When Lynn picked up the letter and gave it to me, her words burned into my head "This is like he is stalking you."

Getting that initial letter made me happy at the time, but eventually I grew to regret getting back in touch with my adoptive father. He hadn't changed his ways. He still belittled me, making me feel that I wasn't capable. I felt mentally abused. I recall when I had my first photo published in the college paper, I had excitedly gone to his office to tell him it would be on the front page. He just nodded his head and countered what I had told him with "Well, I'm going to be on the front page of the newspaper today."

I felt shattered at that rebuttal of an accomplishment I had made. I don't recall words of encouragement, and when I went to visit his house, I still felt out of place and that I was just a guest. I often felt like I had to ask for permission to do things and he would often buy things for me as though the materialistic items would make up for all the trauma that I had experienced with him and his ex-wife.

He never acknowledged his part in the mental and physical abuse that happened in his house, nor said, "I'm sorry for what you went through." I began to wish I had listened to my foster parents and my social worker back in those days, but I hadn't. I thought I knew what was best for me.

I wanted to get back in touch with my adoptive father to find out why my adoptive parents hated me so much that they gave me up and kept my sister.

In the Independant Living Home.

THE SEARCH FOR MY BIRTH MOTHER

Not long after returning to Windsor and starting my college classes, I decided to try to find my birth mom. I wanted to know what she looked like. I wanted to know if she was alive or not. I was tired of riding the buses in the city, seeing other Indigenous women and wondering, "could that be my mom?"

At the time, I didn't know that my mother lived in another province. I guess I hoped that she would magically appear on my doorstep, open her arms, and take me back. I had to go to the very same Children's Aid Society whose authority I was under and talk to a worker by the name of Kathy. I liked Kathy from the start. She was a tall, affable, blonde lady who really listened to you when you talked with her. Her gentleness helped me feel more secure in doing the search for my birth mom. She also was blunt in warning me what I may experience in my search for my mom. "It's not going to be easy," she told me.

Kathy was right—it was not easy. It brought on an avalanche of emotions that I hadn't anticipated. I wasn't sure I could survive them. I had been given conflicting information from my adoptive family about my birth mom and why I was taken away from her and adopted out. They gave me the usual stereotypical notions that non-Indigenous people had of First Nations people. It stung when I heard the words, "she was an unfit mom" or "she was neglectful" and so on. Whatever they told me, it was always her fault that my siblings and I were taken from her.

The burning questions I had about my mom increased tenfold. This didn't help my mental health at all. I suffered from depression and anorexia, but I was determined to keep trying to find my mom. It became an all-consuming project.

Beginning the search for my birth mom was difficult. There were mountains of paperwork to fill out and sometimes I felt like I didn't have the energy to fill out all the papers. I had to put my name on the adoption birth registry saying that if they found my mom, I wanted to have contact with her. I also put my name on the registry to find my birth father and birth siblings.

"Meeting your mom may not work out to be the best thing for you," the social worker told me.

I admit that at the time my ideas about meeting her were grandiose and a bit out in left field. I thought that if I found my mom, all my questions would be answered, and my problems would disappear. I believed that my mom would welcome me back and we would have the greatest relationship in the world.

I knew basic info such as my mom's name, Anna Smith, but I had to research the rest of the information regarding my family. I knew that she lived out of the province of Ontario, and that I had other siblings due to conversations I had with my former adoptive father and his second wife.

My adoptive parents had divorced years earlier, and by the time I came into contact with my adoptive father and his second wife, my sister was living in a second house that my father had bought and fixed up. His sons also lived there, but they have never talked to me. I believe their view of me has been poisoned by what had happened during our childhoods years ago.

The information I sought from my adoptive father was information that was misleading and based in stereotypes that I eventually learned had no basis in fact.

I had periodic meetings with the social worker Kathy to get updates on the progress of my application and in between those meetings I tried to get on with my life. My visits to my foster home in the county became sporadic, and that was no one's fault but my own. I had a lot on my plate emotionally, mentally, spiritually and physically. I was trying to find my mom and my birth family, keeping up with my schoolwork, and dealing with the conflicting emotions of being in touch with my adoptive father again. I was doing my best to cope with depression and the ever-present desire for self-harm. I was cutting myself, my anorexia was worsening, and I was taking pills to numb myself, which led to several overdoses and ending up in the hospital getting my stomach pumped.

The eating disorder I'd been struggling with since age twelve was worse than ever. For some reason I had begun to believe that I wasn't worthy of eating anything and I would stick my fingers down my throat until I thought everything I had tried to eat had been purged from my system. The friends I had didn't know how to deal with what I was doing to myself. They thought that if I just stopped taking pills, or if I just ate and kept it in me, I would be okay. But I wasn't okay, and I didn't understand it myself.

Despite the slippery slope of my eating disorder and depression, I managed to attend school and do my assignments, but the burning questions that were always in the back of my mind—"Is my mom alive? Is she going to want to see me?"—continued to consume me.

By the time I received the notice about my birth mom I had aged out of the Children's Aid Society and was living in a dive of an apartment a block away from the Independent Home where I had previously lived. It had taken more than six months for me to hear back from the adoption registry office. It had been a long wait indeed. I found out as I was on my way to catch the bus to school. I grabbed my mail, ran out of my apartment, and headed towards the bus stop. As I shuffled through the mail, I noticed an official government envelope and immediately felt trepidation as I opened it. My fingers were trembling and my palms were sweaty. This was the moment I had been waiting for, but I wasn't sure what to expect.

I opened the letter and the words I had longed to see jumped out at me:

"YOUR BIRTH MOTHER ANNA SMITH WANTS TO MEET YOU!"

If I had not been crossing the street at the time, I probably would have done a couple of somersaults and whooped and hollered. My heart was pounding with excitement. My mom was alive and wanted to meet me. I would soon meet her. The dream of finding my birth mom was finally becoming reality.

Though it was noted that my birth mother wanted to meet me, I was sad when I found out that my birth father was deceased. He had been murdered.

I also found out that I had an older brother who lived in an institution due to developmental issues and that I had a younger brother who also had been adopted out and was possibly in the United States. Though the news of my birth father dampened some of my excitement, I was still thrilled that I had found my mom, even if it was just on paper for now.

My oldest brother, Billy

AGING OUT OF THE SYSTEM

I was sitting in a cold hard plastic chair off to the side of my social worker's desk at the Children's Aid Society. I had been called in earlier and had taken the city bus to the CAS office.

"You need to come to the office," my social worker Lynn had said. "I have some concerns that I need to speak with you about."

I really didn't want to go. Lynn had been growing more and more distant. She seemed disgusted with how I had been doing at the Independent Living residence that I had moved into upon leaving my last foster home. She didn't tell me that the worker from the residence was going to be there for the meeting.

I walked down a dreary hallway, my eyes squinting as they tried to adjust to the dull yellowish light. I felt apprehensive, which was making my heart pump extra hard, and my palms were sweating because I didn't know why I had been called in. My hands were clenched into fists. I nervously began to clutch each finger and crack my knuckles. The pop... pop... pop... sound was soothing to me. I don't know why. There was a cacophony of voices from other offices, as I walked down the hallway to my worker's office.

After maybe a minute or two I stopped in front of her door. I heard two voices behind the closed door but couldn't make out what they were saying. I took a deep breath and knocked. The wood of the door resounded as my knuckles rapped on the door. There was silence for a couple of seconds, and I heard footsteps. Lynn opened the door, looked at me for a couple of seconds and then said, "Come on in Christine," as she turned and walked back to her desk.

As I followed Lynn into her office, I noticed Laura, the worker from the residence, was sitting at Lynn's desk. I remember gulping and feeling my heart go KA THUMP... KA THUMP... KA THUMP...

I sat down. The chair was cold and unyielding. Lynn and Laura were sitting across from me. Right away, I could tell that this meeting wasn't going to be good. The tension in the air was sharp and palpable. Laura wouldn't look my way, and neither would Lynn. I looked past Lynn's shoulder, and out the huge window behind her. The sun was shining, the birds were chirping, and every once in a while I could hear the sound of cars going by. The office was not far from the parking lot and a busy thoroughfare.

When I had first left my foster home upon graduation from high school and moved back to the city I was adopted into, I thought that things would go well for me. I foolishly believed that in some form or another, independence was the answer to the troubles that plagued me. I was wrong. Instead of feeling free, I became more trapped and more despondent. My mental health at the time was starting to hit a new low.

So, there I was sitting in my social worker's office, and in front of her were bottles of medication that she had received from Laura, the worker at the Independent Living House. The medication had been taken from my room. I don't recall how many bottles were there, maybe four or five, maybe more. Between the two of them, they had opened the bottles and had spilled the pills out onto the desk that lay between them. They started counting "1... 2... 3... 4... 5... 6... " and as they counted, they looked up at me to see if I was watching.

"Do you really have to do that?" I yelled.

I remember sitting in that chair, my face flushing with anger, my arms crossed over my chest and slightly rocking myself back and forth, back and forth. I was shivering too. It could have been from the fact that I hadn't eaten anything, or it could have been the anxiety I felt, as they sat there doing what I thought was them colluding against me.

The pills they were counting included my antidepressants, Tylenol, anti-anxiety meds, and laxatives. I had stockpiled them in my drawer at the Independent Living Home. As they continued to count out loud, I grew more and more infuriated until finally the anger that was brewing inside me burst.

"I hate you, Lynn! I hate the Children's Aid, I hate the house I'm living in, and I wish you both would just leave me alone."

"Christine, you need to calm down," Lynn said.

"I'm not going to calm down!" I yelled back. "I'm sick of you guys!"

After a couple of minutes of yelling, I felt spent from my outburst, and slouched back into my chair, glowering at Lynn and Laura.

"Christine," Lynn said, "you have two weeks to find an apartment and then you won't have to worry about being with us anymore."

I shook my head to see if I heard her correctly.

Lynn repeated it again, "Christine, you have two weeks to find an apartment. Then you won't have to worry about being with the Children's Aid anymore."

I couldn't believe what I was hearing. I looked at her with shock. After a couple of seconds, I said, "Fine!"

I left my CAS worker's office after our exchange. The two of them were still counting my pills as I slammed the office door behind me. I remember walking back down that hallway at breakneck speed. I felt tears start streaming down my face. Tears always seemed to come when I got angry. I left the CAS building as soon as I could. I remember I didn't head straight back to the group home right away. I wandered around and around and didn't care where I was or what people thought as I furiously wiped at the tears that just didn't want to stop. I was angry that I had let myself lose control like that and yell at my social worker.

I don't recall how long I wandered around; it was probably a couple of hours but eventually the sun started to go down. It was getting chillier and growing darker by the second. I finally headed back to the group home, where I went directly to my room, closed the door, and collapsed on top of my bed. I fell into a fitful sleep, not knowing what the next day would bring.

A day or two later, I began to search for an apartment. At seventeen years old, I didn't know how to rent an apartment or what to look for in the ads. I just knew that I had very little time to find a place, before I had to be out of the group home.

I pored over newspaper advertisements and called a handful of places. In between calls, I packed my meager belongings—a few stuffed animals, my pillow, my clothes, some books and paper, my music cassettes and ghetto blaster, and a small television. I don't recall how long it took after the outburst I had at my social worker's office, but I finally found an apartment.

The apartment was down the street from the group home. It was a bachelor apartment that went for a little over two hundred and fifty dollars, and social assistance helped me with that. It had a big main room, a fair-sized bathroom with an old-fashioned tub, and a small kitchen. The apartment was situated off the parking lot of an unsavoury bar, and the apartment itself had little guests that I had never encountered before—cockroaches.

The first time I saw a cockroach in my apartment was when I was in my kitchen, trying to make soup. I had a ladle in my hand when I happened to glance up at the shelf above my head. I saw two little antennas and beady little eyes looking at me.

"AAHH!" I screeched.

Has this bloody cockroach been there all this time staring at me? I wondered.

I lost my appetite and left the soup sitting on the stove. I walked out of the kitchen and sat on my bed. I remember feeling disgusted that my life had come to this—living in a cockroach-infested apartment, with noisy neighbours who were always yelling, fighting, and throwing things around. I remember the fear I felt every time I heard the resounding thump of something hitting up against my wall. I often lay in my bed trembling and thinking not only that something bad was going to happen to my neighbours but that something bad was going to happen to me too.

These thoughts were not far-fetched. After living there for a year, I gave my notice to my landlord, and it wasn't long after I moved out that I heard there had been a murder in that apartment building. One of the neighbours I had heard yelling and fighting had killed his partner in a domestic assault.

Life on my own was definitely a test that CAS hadn't prepared me for. At seventeen years old, you're still a kid, whether you care to believe it or not. You think that you can take on the world and everyone and everything in it. I didn't realize that by essentially getting kicked out of the Children's Aid, I would be on my own and would have to learn things such as how to furnish my own place, cook, pay rent and pay bills. I had to be responsible for myself, whereas before I had always had someone watching out for me. I was a child at heart thrust into a world I didn't know how to navigate.

IT BEGAN WITH A COMMENT

My eating disorder began with taunting from a classmate when I was in eighth grade and living at my last foster home in Kingsville, and it would take years before I could release myself from its all-consuming hold on me.

As one of only two foster kids in a small town that was predominantly white, I was teased mercilessly. My shyness was ridiculed and the fact that the teachers went out of their way to make me feel comfortable left me wide open for teasing from the other kids. I was called a teacher's pet, amongst other things. My foster parents didn't know about the turmoil I felt inside and what I endured in my classes and from my classmates. I wish I had told them, but for some reason I kept it inside.

Then one day, one comment changed everything.

"Look at you! You're so fat, you can't fit into your desk."

In my classroom, the desks were small, and I fit into them fine, but the comment devastated me. The girl who made the comment was the type of girl I wanted to be like. She was pretty, popular, thin and a straight A student. I was the new kid who came into the class halfway through the school year, and I was the only First Nations kid, in a sea of white faces, in a primarily white school and town.

She and other kids made comments that intensified my already insecure sense of self. In retrospect, I didn't know how to deal with the comments or treatment from my peers. I didn't understand it at the time but I tried to cope by controlling my intake of food. It began with cutting back foods that I normally enjoyed. This meant no peanut butter and bread, no chips, no ice cream, and no fried foods. I said good-bye to a lot of foods, without really understanding why.

My foster parents were perplexed at what I was doing. One day while we were having a conversation on the deck in their backyard, my foster mom nonchalantly asked me, "What's wrong Christine? Why aren't you eating?"

I told her, "I have to watch what I take in."

"Why?" she asked.

I could not give a clear explanation. I didn't understand it myself.

I started making lists of foods that I couldn't touch. I wrote them in my journal every night. The list kept getting bigger and bigger, and it became a list that I absolutely had to live by. Crazy rules popped into my head, like not eating any foods that were mixed together, not eating anything with sauces, and not using condiments. If I wanted pop, I could only have diet pop. I refused to drink any milk. Desserts were definitely a huge no-no.

Keeping my list straight in my head was taxing and often had me spinning. If I went off my list, I blamed myself for loss of self-control and punished myself by taking in fewer calories than I had taken in the meal before or by going up to the washroom and purging everything that I had consumed—whether that was through making myself vomit or drinking a bottle of Milk of Magnesia. I also used water pills and laxatives if I could find them.

I didn't know how to voice the pain I felt from what I was experiencing at school or the behaviours I was engaging in through my eating disorder. Anorexia consumed me for the remainder of my stay in my last foster home, and it continued long after I had left foster care and was on my own.

I went from being relatively quiet and sharp to someone who became more withdrawn, moody, and a shadow of my former self. Essentially my spirit disappeared.

Mealtimes became fraught with anxiety. My foster parents at the time didn't know what to make of what I was doing, but they tried to accommodate me with things they knew I would eat. While my foster parents Lois and Gary, their son Doug, and my foster sister Tanya would have a heaping plate of spaghetti or potatoes and meat, I would sit at the table with a bowl of plain rice, twirling my fork around the bowl, and taking tiny bites. Rice quickly became a staple at every meal; it was what I called a "safe food." In my early days with anorexia nervosa, a safe food was one that I didn't have the desire to get rid of it as soon as it hit my mouth.

Anorexia nervosa consumed me for the remainder of my stay in my foster home. I feel shame at the measures my foster parents had to take with me—locking their freezer with a big lock so that their popsicles wouldn't disappear. The absurdity in that was that I thought that if I just ate a popsicle, it would sustain me. They had to hide their Milk of Magnesia and their occasional boxes of laxatives and water pills because they never knew when I would reach into the medicine cabinet and take them, and with my emotions all over the place, and the tantrums I threw, they occasionally had to hold me down so that I wouldn't hurt myself or anyone else around me.

The transition of moving from place to place and getting used to new people was part of the turmoil I was feeling, but I didn't realize how much my inner pain and confusion contributed to this eating disorder. When I left my foster home, I remember promising a couple of friends that I would be back to visit, and yes, I did go back and visit a few times, but that slowly stopped when I started to withdraw within myself.

Being away from the friends I had made was also difficult to say the least. Going from a foster home that offered structure and having people around me to living on my own was difficult. It tests your very being. I look back now and ask myself, *How did I do it?*

When I think that after a childhood of moving from foster home to foster home, I had to live on my own at such a young age and without any preparation by the CAS, it makes me determined to tell my stories in the hopes that other Indigenous youth won't have to go through what I did.

I wish that at the time there had been programs to help me to make the transition from being in care to being on my own. I also wish that I had listened to those who tried to advise me back then about what could happen living on my own, and how I could have dealt with the issues that I was facing. If I had known any better, which I can now admit that at the age of seventeen I didn't, I would not have allowed myself to be kicked out of the Independent Living group home I had been in. I would have tried to accept the help that was offered to me and I wouldn't have become reliant upon social assistance.

Not all foster kids choose what happens to them when they leave the system. I certainly didn't. Because of some life experiences, some kids need more support than others, and they may need it for longer. In my case, after several years of relying on my former adoptive father for periodic help, I was left floundering on my own. I fell into debt. Slowly, I began to build a support system around me. It was a little crazy, because I had workers for everything imaginable at first. After a few hospitalizations, I was put under the financial guardianship of the Ontario Public Guardian and Trustee office.

Being under a trustee meant that there was a government employee who controlled all aspects of my financial obligations. It was difficult at first, but I do admit that it stopped me from falling through the cracks of a system I often felt was out to destroy me. I can't take back the years I spent floundering, but I do thank the various workers in the mental health and social work field who took the time to teach me the things they did even when I had my back up in anger and defiance and didn't want to listen. The knowledge that they passed on has helped me in ways they could never know. I am fortunate that I was a foster kid who was able to turn her life around.

TORONTO BOUND

After many years in Windsor, I decided to move four hours away—to Toronto. Windsor was a place that constantly reminded me of the trauma and pain I had gone through, not only as a child, but also as a teenager trying to make her way after transitioning out of the child welfare system. The decision wasn't easy, but I knew in my heart that I had to do something because if I didn't, I wasn't sure what would happen to me emotionally, mentally, physically and spiritually.

A social worker by the name of Dominic from the Sandwich Community Health Centre moved me to Toronto. The first place I stayed in was the Toronto General Hospital Residence building. Before leaving Windsor, I had signed up for treatment with the National Eating Disorder Clinic. My treatment there was fraught with difficulties that I brought on myself. At first, I complied with the meal plans they put me on, and went to the counselling sessions, but after a while I grew defiant and wanted to leave. I acted out in ways that I became ashamed of but not until after I was asked to leave the eating disorder program.

Not long after I left the program, I moved from the Toronto General Hospital Residence, and into the YWCA. Living with others was difficult for me, and after moving around to a few shared places, I finally struck out and got my own place. For some reason, I found that I could never stay at a place longer than a year. Annually, I would look for another place, move in, make it my home, and then pull up and move again. I never really understood the desire to pick up and move all the time. I went from living in residences, shared homes with roommates, spending time in shelters when I felt I couldn't cope on my own, and then finally living on my own.

Living on my own at this time became a freedom like nothing else I had experienced, and I learned to love it. There was just something about having no rules, no one to answer to, and calling my own shots that I loved.

Toronto became my home. I slowly built my own community and support system and finally felt a semblance of peace and contentment.

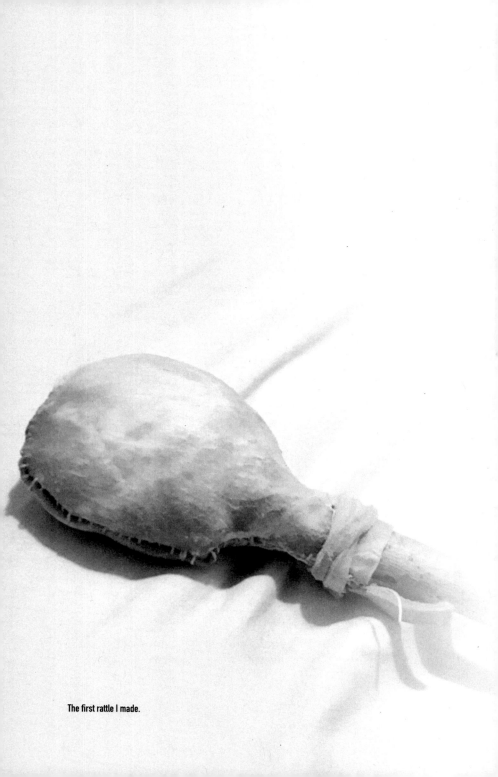

The first rattle I made.

SOMETHING IS EATING AWAY AT ME

The shout out "It's dinner time!" used to be the three words I dreaded the most. I remember sitting on my bed, hunched over my night table furiously colouring in the book I had bought at the hospital gift store on one of my trips off the psychiatric ward.

I want to ignore the call out, but know that if I do, my doctor will be told that I am being difficult. I put my markers away in their plastic wrap and put them down on the table where my poster lay. I swing my legs over the edge of my bed and stand up. I feel a wave of dizziness; I stop, grab the table beside me and close my eyes until it passes.

I walk slowly out of the room, pulling my sweater around me closely, as I feel the cold from the hospital's A/C system, and shiver. I try not to pay attention to the scurrying of the other patients around me, as they head into the dining room.

I hear the attendant start to call out the patient's names and room numbers. "801A, 801B, 801C"

I don't have to sit with everyone. My doctor has decided that the nurses need to keep an eye on me. He wants me behind the nurses' desk, so that they can see whether I am eating or not. I try to tell myself that I don't like this arrangement, but secretly I do because it means that I don't have to be near anyone else. I like being alone, separated from everyone else, because then I won't have to hear the comments from the other patients.

"Christine, why aren't you eating?"

"I'll take your food, if you're not going to eat it."

I don't want people taking my food. It is my food, even if I'm not going to touch it.

I pull out the cold plastic chair that's in front of me and sit down. I look at the tray in front of me and mentally go over what I'll try to eat and what I won't touch. Food occupies my mind ninety per cent of my waking hours. The other ten percent is how I can fool others around me into believing that I'm trying to get better and that I'm going to start eating. Food is my enemy.

I have been in the hospital this time for over a month. When I got admitted; the nurses shook their heads and said, "Christine, you have to stop this, you have to start eating."

"You want to get, better don't you?" they would ask.

I couldn't explain to anyone why I was so afraid to eat. I just knew that this disorder—anorexia nervosa—had begun with the rationing and monitoring of food from my time at my adoptive family's house.

Sitting in the cold plastic chair behind the nurse's desk, I look at the food on my tray. I wrinkle my nose when I see that it consists of a salad, soup, and goop they call macaroni and cheese. One of the nurses comes up and stands beside my chair. I feel her hand come down upon my shoulder and I look up at her as she says, "Christine, at least eat the salad."

I nod my head at her; I can feel the tears threatening to spill. I grab the closest utensil, and as the nurse turns to walk away, I eat one piece of lettuce, and grimace. To me, this is torture.

Long hospital stays were the norm for me in the throes of my eating disorder. The doctors were also treating me for post-traumatic stress disorder and depression. The hospital served as my refuge from the chaos I felt on the inside and on the outside. Today, after much hard work, I am free from that confined refuge.

Treatment was often difficult no matter where I was because I often fought to comply with what my doctors and therapists were trying to teach me. Over the course of being in and out of in-patient and out-patient treatment, I came across a catalogue called Gurze Books, and though the place was based in California, I gave one of the co-founders a call, because the husband-and-wife team were specialists in the eating disorders field. Lindsey Hall-Cohn was a survivor herself and had been in active recovery from bulimia nervosa for over twenty years.

Lindsey Hall-Cohn and Leigh Cohn, even though they lived in California, helped me immensely by giving me the unconditional love I had yearned for all my life—never leaving even when things got difficult, teaching me to reexamine my thinking when I needed to and reframe my thoughts from negative into positive. They offered me the strong support and encouragement that I required, and introduced me to how I could be with my difficult feelings and emotions and allow myself the permission to nurture myself the way I had needed to when I was younger. They taught me topics such as healthy boundaries, self-care and journalling amongst many other skills that helped me want to be in recovery. They entered my life after an initial telephone call and have become my greatest friends and allies. Over many years, through phone calls, letters, and email, Lindsey Hall-Cohn and Leigh Cohn offered me the love I had always yearned for, and the support to help guide me to the recovery point I am at today. I have even gone to visit them and treasure those visits like no others.

Though I believe that food will always be an issue for me, and it's something that I will always have to be conscious about, I am no longer in the throes of an eating disorder that could very well have killed me. Instead, I am here today, smiling and saying, "Chi miigwetch"

I have my life back.

My first multi-media painting, untitled.

I JUST WANTED SOMEONE TO KNOW I WAS HURTING

"Christine, you can't give up. You have to keep fighting," says the warm, calming voice through the phone line. The voice belongs to the director at the Crisis Centre that I seem to be on the phone with daily these days.

He gets paid to say this to me, I think to myself. I know deep down that's not true, but the thought flits around my head. My head feels heavy, and my eyes are tired. I'm in my apartment in Windsor, twirling a piece of hair around my finger, as I speak.

"I just can't take this depression anymore. I don't know what is causing it," I tell the man on the other end of the phone. "I just can't cope anymore."

I sniff really loudly, and gulp as I try to calm my heart from beating so fast. We're past the point of him asking me what it is that has brought me to tears today. He is more concerned that I am about to hurt myself again.

"I'm glad you called, Christine," he says. "Can you keep yourself safe?

There is silence for a second before his voice breaks through again.

"Tell me the things you can do to keep yourself safe."

Like a robot, I hear myself repeat the things therapy has taught me over and over again. "I can go for a walk, take a bubble bath, call someone, write, read, or wait… wait…" My voice trails off as I begin to cry. "I've called you, and I'm not calming down!

Fresh tears begin again. The director from the Crisis Centre has the patience of Job. He is quiet for a couple of seconds.

"Christine, breathe, breathe," he tells me. "You are going to be okay."

"I don't think I will be this time," I tell him.

"I need to know that you are going to keep yourself safe, Christine," he says. "Or I will have to call an ambulance."

Though his voice has always been the calm in the storm, I hear myself tell him, "I have to go… I have to go, bye."

I don't think about how I have left the conversation, or if I have worried anyone. I let the phone drop back into its cradle, and I crawl back to the futon that serves a dual function—by day, my sofa and by night, my bed. I collapse on it. My thin trembling body curls up in the fetal position. My knees are drawn close, and my arms are wrapped tightly around them. I pull the blanket haphazardly around me, as the tears course down my face like a waterfall.

RING… RING… RING… I ignore the phone and pull my pillow over my head to dim the sound. I don't know how long I have lain there; I just know that I can't take this despair anymore. Nothing has really set it off, it's a part of my daily life. Other than my therapist, and my friends in California, no one else really understands this illness. They have grown impatient with me, because I am either crying all the time or isolating myself.

I've been crying for what seems like hours, and I am so damn tired.

No one wants to be around someone as moody as this, I tell myself. *Everyone will be better off without me.*

My head spins as I sit up. I can't remember when I last ate. I grab the scissors. The blanket falls from my shoulders as I groggily sit up, one hand wiping at my face, while the other grasps the scissors. Balancing precariously on the edge of my bed, I make a swift swipe.

I feel the initial sting as the scissors make their mark. My eyes take in the angry welts that are beginning to show on my forearm. I see my blood slowly pop up in thin red lines and I feel a sense of relief come over me. The cuts aren't that deep; they're mere scratches on my arm but the blood makes the cuts looks worse than they really are. *I can hide these with long sleeves*, I think to myself.

I get up and slowly walk to my kitchen and grab a paper towel. I apply it to my arm and then head back to my futon to lie back down. As I start to lie down, I see a bottle of Tylenol beside my bed. I think about taking some, because for some reason, the cuts I've made on my arm are not enough to take away the pain I'm feeling. It's tempting, but fatigue wins, and I leave the bottle sitting on my night table. I think of calling the Crisis Centre again, but when I glance at the clock, I see that their day would be over. It's 5 p.m. I bunch up my pillow underneath my head, pull my blankets around myself, and drift into a fitful sleep.

Suddenly, I'm jolted awake by a BANG… BANG… BANG… followed by a deep gravelly voice shouting.

"Christine! … Christine! … Are you in there?"

There's a pause.

"I'm coming in."

I hear the key turn in the lock, and look up. My landlord rushes into my apartment. Two paramedics follow him.

"Christine," says one of the paramedics, "what did you do? We got a phone call from someone called Bob from the Crisis Centre saying he was concerned about you."

Looking up from underneath my covers, I mutter, "Nothing, it doesn't matter."

"Yes, it does, Christine. Come on. What did you do?" he repeats. The paramedic comes closer to my bed but stops before he reaches my side.

"Do you have any weapons on you right now that can hurt you or anyone else?" he asks.

"No," I tell him.

My landlord is standing at the side looking over at me. He's shaking his head, as one of the paramedics gently pulls the covers away from me and asks me to sit up. He sees the paper towel and the blood on it.

"Did you cut yourself?" he asks.

I nod my head. Too tired to speak. The other paramedic is looking around my living room, presumably for other things I might have used to hurt myself. The paramedic by my side pulls out a blood pressure cuff.

"Put out your arm, Christine," he says. "I have to check your blood pressure, and take your pulse."

He turns to my landlord. "We're going to take her to the hospital to get her some help," he says.

My landlord nods his head. The other paramedic strides across the floor, and they both put their hands under my elbows and walk me to the stretcher that sits outside my apartment door. They help me onto the stretcher, and I lie down. Because I am shivering, they pull a thin orange blanket over me. They wheel the stretcher to the elevator a few feet away and then out the main door of the building. Once I am ensconced in the back of the ambulance, with a paramedic sitting beside me, the door slams shut, and the sirens start. Minutes later, I'm wheeled into the ER.

I'm sitting on the gurney waiting for the doctor, my fingers picking at the well-worn corners of the sheet underneath me. A nurse comes in briefly to check my vitals.

"The doctor will be in shortly," the nurse says.

What seems like hours of waiting is only about forty-five minutes. The doctor comes in. "Hello Christine," the doctor says. "What brings you here today?"

For a few minutes we talk.

"This is happening too much," he says. "We're going to find you a bed and admit you. For now, we're going to give you something to help you calm down and then you'll go up to the psych ward."

I nod my head and feel thankful that my cries have at last been heard.

This hospital admission was one of many during my early years of battling depression. I often walked around in a haze, if I made it out of my bed at all. If I wasn't doped up on medication or in the hospital, I was at home. I rarely laughed and the tears seemed endless. I remember that I often wondered what the hell was wrong with me. It took years of therapy and many courses of medication before I realized that I suffered from a mental illness and that if it went untreated it would surely have landed me six feet under.

No one at that time really understood those despairing feelings that made me want to hurt myself, and if someone had ever asked me, I'm sure that I wouldn't have been able to speak about what it was that made me want to abuse myself. Cutting served as an outlet and let the world know, "Hey, I'm hurting!"

I carry faint scars on my arms from that time. It's not something that I am proud of. It reminds me of the abuse I put myself through, whether that was cutting, starving myself, or taking pills. It reminds me of the abuse I experienced at the hands of my adoptive parents and how, through no fault of my own, I was continuing that abuse on myself. The darkness of my depression allowed me to hurt myself because I thought that I deserved it.

Before I moved to Toronto, the hospital served as a safe haven, a place where I knew I could be saved from the torment going on within my mind. I didn't know that once I worked through the torment that drove me to the ER, I would become free. Like an eagle, I have grown wings and risen up from the darkness. I have learned that it is okay to honour my feelings, express myself through words and art, and ask for help when I need it. This allows me to be gentler with myself, at last.

MY AWAKENING

My life has been filled with many experiences, some good and some bad, but one of these experiences has been what I would call my awakening within. It encompasses many things but, in my awakening, I have learned through my writing to embrace who I am—a First Nations woman deserving of a voice and a successful life.

As a child of the '60s and '70s scoop, when First Nations children were adopted out into non-native families by the assimilationist policies of the Canadian government, I grew up immersed in a culture that was not my own. I was a First Nations child who did not know how to live in both worlds—the non-Indigenous world and the First Nations world.

Because I was not allowed to draw upon my heritage in any way, I grew up in ignorance of my people. I became very judgmental and hateful towards not only myself but towards the people who made up my community. In part this was because it had been instilled in me for so many years that somehow being First Nations meant that there was *something wrong with me.*

This void that grew within came from repeatedly being told by my adoptive parents that there was something wrong with me and that nothing I did would ever amount to anything. I never considered that the people telling me these things were the ones who were sick themselves. To fill the void, I learned many dysfunctional ways to deal with the hurt and trauma that I experienced at the hands of my adoptive parents. I learned to be silent, fearful, and anxious. I learned to use disordered eating and self-harm behaviours to numb myself from learning who I really was as an individual.

Living in Toronto and having the support system that I slowly built around me was what saved me. I learned from workers who took great interest in helping me to shape my own identity. I learned that breaking away from those in the past who had hurt me could set me free. I learned by adopting a path of re-discovery of the culture that had been denied to me. I learned through ceremony, tradition, being a part of the First Nations community and through my writing that I have a voice that matters. Writing has always fascinated me. It plays a huge part in my healing and recovery and has been instrumental in how I see myself today.

As a teen and young adult, I always had some type of notebook to write in, and I collected pens. It was as though I could never have enough paper or pens for my writing. People would tease me about the books and pens that I collected, but they did not know that in a way I was gathering the courage to tell the stories that I wanted so desperately to share with the world.

The art of writing has been an instrumental way for me to stay strong and to have the courage to keep on going. When I first began to write, I treated the process as though it was my only friend, and meticulously poured out my thoughts through journal writing, poetry, inspirational prose, and short stories. The process became a way of life for me, a way to express myself in a way that was a safety net for me. I continue to write now, not only for myself but for others too.

In telling my story and sharing my experiences, I am hoping that those who have had similar experiences do not feel alone like I did for much of my young life. I have found healing in my writing and in my healing, I have awakened within.

THE FIRST VISIT WITH MY BIRTH MOM

After a flurry of phone calls from a repatriation worker who had tracked me down by telephone in Toronto, it was arranged for me to head to Winnipeg to meet my birth mom. My memory is a bit blurry about how long it took to make this visit—it might have been a few months after the initial call from the repatriation worker—but I travelled for three days on a Greyhound bus from Toronto to meet my biological mother. At that time, my mom was living in Saskatchewan with her partner. For our first visit, she came from Saskatchewan into Winnipeg.

When we arrived at the bus terminal, my body was aching from hours of sitting or flopping over two cramped seats to try to get some sleep. When the bus lurched into the station, I exited the bus, grabbed my bags, and slowly made my way into the station.

My mom was standing in the station beside a repatriation worker. I don't recall his name, but his demeanor was uppity and cocky, as though he would rather be anywhere else but here, watching a woman meet her grown daughter for the very first time.

My heart leapt into my throat as I entered the station and looked across the stained and worn plastic seats and saw a woman who looked just like me.

She was short, even shorter than the five feet that I am. She was bundled up for the Winnipeg cold—they don't call it "Winterpeg" for nothing. Her hair was black like mine, but hers was salt-and-pepper with grey running through it. Like me, she wore glasses. They were pretty thick. I had to laugh; I must have gotten my bad eyesight from her. I'd worn glasses since I was ten years old.

It was crazy to go to Winnipeg in the middle of winter, but I had been waiting almost thirty-two years to see what my mother actually looked like, and I would not have missed it for the world. There are no words to explain the feelings that coursed through me when I saw her for the first time. I was speechless. I finally had a living, breathing person in front of me. Finally, after years of wondering and imagining, I knew what Anna Smith looked like. She was real and she was standing in front of me.

The tears rolled down her cheeks and she clumsily reached out to put her arms around me. I wasn't used to hugs. I gave her a hug back, but it was awkward. I didn't know what to say or do to calm her down. Nor did I know that before I got there she had been pacing back and forth and asking herself the very same questions that I had. "Will she look like me?" Will she like me?" "What if she hates me and doesn't want anything to do with me?"

The three of us left the bus station. My mom and I had our arms around each other. Everything was surreal. We were really in each other's presence. The little girl in me was crying, but the grown woman on the outside was stoic. *You have to be strong*, I told myself.

My mom and I didn't do a lot on the first day of our visit. We had been dropped off at the Regis Hotel in downtown Winnipeg, and after getting us checked in, the repatriation worker left. The room wasn't anything to write home about—a mustiness hit my nostrils as soon as I opened the door. There was a worn brown carpet throughout the room, two king beds, and a heavy curtain that blocked out the light. The door was so thin that you hear every sound coming from the hallway—people coming and going and the elevator doors opening and closing.

I put my stuff on an overstuffed chair by the window.

"I'll take the bed by the window," I told my mom.

My mom took the other bed that was close to the door. I recall sitting on my bed and my mom sitting on hers, and talking. Our conversation was pretty awkward. I don't recall what we talked about, but I remember the moments of silence.

I felt overwhelmed and decided to call a friend back in Toronto. Afterwards my mom was sitting at the edge of her bed snacking on an orange. She turned to me.

"Did you want some orange?" she asked.

"No thank you."

A few minutes later, my mom fell to the floor. I could hear her gurgling. I remember rushing to her side, and her twitching on the floor.

"What's wrong Mom? What's wrong?" I kept asking her over and over again.

I crouched down beside her, and when I did, I saw some orange in her mouth. I felt a sudden surge of energy inside me. Although I had never taken a First Aid course, I turned my mom on her side, opened her mouth and pulled out a piece of orange that might have been blocking her airway.

I sat with her for a couple of seconds but she was twitching and I realized she wasn't getting any better. I ran to the hotel room phone and called the front desk.

"I need an ambulance, my mom is choking," I screamed.

While the hotel desk clerk called an ambulance two total strangers who heard the commotion knocked on the door and offered to help. They helped me to stay calm, and my mom to stay calm, while we waited for the ambulance to come. When I heard the ambulance approaching the hotel, it took all my strength and courage not to break down crying. I hated ambulances, because of my own experiences, and I wasn't sure if my mom had had experiences with them. It felt like forever before the ambulance attendants knocked on the door, but when they did, for once I welcomed it. I let them in, and they went to work right away.

As they worked on my mom, taking her pulse, checking her blood pressure, they grilled me about what happened. I told them about the orange and how she had put a piece in her mouth and then suddenly had fallen.

I told them that I had put her on her side and taken extra pieces of orange out of her mouth.

"That was a great move," one EMT said.

They put my mom on a stretcher and covered her in a bright orange blanket. I stood by my mom's side.

"You'll be okay," I kept telling her. "You'll be okay."

As the ambulance attendants left with my mom on the stretcher, I grabbed my purse.

"I'm going with her," I said. The elevator seemed to move slowly, but once I hopped into the ambulance, I felt some relief. The ambulance ride was intense but thank goodness it was quick. We pulled into the Women's Health Science Centre and my mom was taken in right away.

I tried to answer some questions from one of the nurses.

"Did you cause your mom to get into this condition?" the nurse actually had the audacity to ask me.

My jaw dropped when I heard that question. I told the nurse that I didn't know the history of my mom's health because that day was the first day that we had seen each other. The nurse became quiet.

"You can go in and see her," she told me.

Going into the emergency room brought back memories of all the times I had been rushed into emergency, and the treatment I had received there. It brought back memories of the time the hospital had to call my sister Marguerite to tell her, "Your sister has flatlined."

I couldn't imagine the pain that my sister had felt at hearing that, but it made me feel guilty. The image of my mom lying on her bed, and twitching, and the nurses strapping her down made me want to just crash to the floor and cry. But I didn't.

I went out into the waiting room and sat down. I had a couple of telephone numbers with me. I don't remember when or where I got them, but they were the numbers of my aunt and one of my uncles. I called my Uncle Peter, and told him what was happening. Then I called my aunt Shirley and told her the same thing. They told me they would be there within an hour or so. I later realized that they had been in the city so that they could come to meet me and my mom.

The emergency room wait went by more quickly than I expected. After a couple of hours, the doctor told me that my mom had had a seizure caused by the stress she had been feeling about our first visit. I had left my mom's side briefly to speak to the doctor, but was going to sit with her again. One of my mom's nurses said it would be better if I waited for a little while in the waiting room. I felt butterflies in my stomach. My head was spinning.

I did what the nurses requested. Sitting in the cold, unyielding chairs, I waited for my aunt and uncle to show up. It seemed like I sat there for a couple of hours, but it could have been longer. The rest of that first day was a blur. But I do remember my mom all of a sudden coming out of the emergency room, and the mother and daughter roles becoming reversed.

When my mom came out of the ER, she quietly said, "We can go now." I looked over my mom quickly, and before I got up from my seat, I zipped up her coat. As we stood, my Uncle Peter came through the hospital's emergency room door. I think we took a taxi back to the Regis Hotel and went to our room for the rest of the day.

This first visit with my mom was only for three days. During that time, I met my aunt Shirley and my uncles Peter and Sam. I remember at some point, my mom and I rushing through the severe cold to a woman's apartment. My mom told me it was a friend of hers. We had maybe one visit like that, but most of the time we were in the hotel room, and didn't venture far. My mom was proud of me and talking to me with my uncles and my aunt. She told me that I had two brothers, Billy and Victor. In order, my mom had my older brother Billy, my sister Doreen Marguerite (later switched to Marguerite), me and then my younger brother, Victor. My mom was never able to find Victor, and neither was I. Victor is still lost.

On that visit I didn't ask her how she dealt with the pain so many years ago when the Children's Aid Society swooped in and took all four of her kids. I didn't think that all the pain would resurface on its own and become so overwhelming it would land her in the hospital, not only while we were visiting, but afterwards when she took the bus back to Saskatchewan and was alone once more. She stayed six weeks in the psychiatric ward.

Five years after that visit, there were many questions that still remained unanswered. We went for a time not seeing each other because it was difficult for me to travel to Manitoba to see her, and we didn't always have a way to get a hold of each other. When we couldn't reach each other, I remembered her nervous laugh and how she would break out humming when there was a loss for words between us on the telephone. It made me laugh and smile. I wanted to break out into song too.

I remembered our first visit and the subsequent visit when I travelled out to Saskatchewan where she had moved with her partner, and then the visits when my mom and her partner moved back to the province of Manitoba.

There were things said on various visits that hurt me. One of those things was when my stepdad Jim told me my birth father had "died like a dog in the street." Those words stung because my dad was murdered, and no one deserves to have their life taken. Things also happened on a few of my visits, things I had never really been through before. I remember Jim's friend, though married, had clumsily hugged me and drunkenly told me I was "really hot." The amount of drinking scared me but I kept that inside too.

When I visited my mom in Saskatchewan, I witnessed her drink bottles of cough syrup when her feelings got to be too much. When she wasn't gulping down cough syrup, she was sleeping on that couch of hers. She rarely left it. Once I asked her to bake cookies with me.

"Do it yourself," she said, turned around, and slept some more.

I felt alone but couldn't say anything. I didn't want to get her all worked up. I saw my mom as somewhat fragile, but as I got to know her, I learned she was anything but fragile. Though she appeared meek, she was strong, and she was a survivor of horrors that no one should have to go through.

At the age of twelve, my mom had told me she was sent by my grandma to the store to get some milk. I think it was back on the reserve, but my mom never really went into much detail. My mom did as she was asked, but when she got back home she found my grandma's body on the floor—she was dead. She had been murdered.

My mom was a Residential School survivor. She attended Brandon Residential School and Birtle Residential School. I cannot even begin to imagine the abuse she went through at these schools. I tried to look up these schools to find some information on them because I didn't dare ask my mom what happened while she was there.

I do remember when I visited my mom in Ashern, Manitoba that we went to see an auntie of hers—my great auntie. This auntie's name was also Anna. She was a petite woman, and I could tell she had been through a lot also. What touched me the most was when she gave me the biggest hug she could and said, "Welcome home!"

Auntie Anna later told me that not many Sixties Scoop children made it back home. She left me with a searing image in my mind that I'll never forget. She told me about when the children were taken from the reserve and herded into the backs of trucks. I'll never forget what she said–"the children were treated like animals."

The image of children staring out of the back of a truck as they were taken from what they knew—their community, family, and culture—will never leave my mind.

BACK TO SCHOOL IN MY THIRTIES

Something switched on in my head in 2004, when one particular social worker named Darlene took an interest in my well-being and what I wanted to do with my life. Darlene was my support worker for about a year, and she had worked steadily with me to gain my trust. Part of her job was as a crisis worker, and another part of her job had her taking me to appointments, going for a coffee with me, and talking about and helping me with other things that cropped up.

Over time our visits became more than just about getting things done like adjusting to new situations, learning how to grocery shop, and getting new clothes. This worker became a friend who outside of her daily work with me would take the time to sit and listen to me. She would calm me when I was having an anxiety attack or feeling particularly low and wanting to hurt myself.

"I want to change," I would tell her.

"Why can't you?" she would ask.

Often when she asked me that, I would shrug my shoulders, say "I don't know," and look down at my lap.

My life up until my decision to head back to school was filled with uncertainties. I was in and out of crisis centres, hospitals, and group therapy, had one crisis worker after another, and was legally put under the Ontario Public Guardian And Trustee Office because I was unable to handle my own affairs. I was a lost soul who could have fallen through the cracks if someone hadn't taken the time to listen, care, and help me act on what would ultimately change my life.

Darlene knew that I didn't really have anyone I could confide in. I didn't have any friends until Darlene walked with me through the doors of the Native Canadian Friendship Centre and had me ask about volunteering. I remember the fear I felt when I went to the front desk. My fear melted when the receptionist, a very friendly older lady with big grey braids, whose name I learned was Barb looked up with a big smile.

"Welcome to the Native Canadian Centre," she said. "How can I help you?"

I looked at her shyly and mumbled, "I want to know about volunteering here."

"That's great!" she replied. "Go up the main stairs here, and to your right you will find the membership and volunteer office. Ask to speak to Lorie, she's in charge of volunteers here. She can help you out."

"Um, thank you," I said, and I turned around. Darlene had been standing off to the side, and I looked over at her and she nodded her head at me, acknowledging the anxiety I was feeling inside. As I looked away from Darlene and slowly made the trek up the stairs, my heart was pounding. I wanted to turn around and run. I could feel the beads of sweat on my forehead, but I didn't run. Instead, I forged ahead.

The door to the volunteer/membership office was open, and there were a few people bustling around. One person was on the computer, another was on the phone and another was shuffling through some papers. I quietly knocked on the worn-down door and waited for a second or two. A lady looked up and smiled.

"Hello," she said. " Can I help you?
"I was sent up here from the front desk to ask about volunteering. Are you Lorie?" I replied.

"Yes, yes I am," she said. She got up from behind her desk and made her way across the cluttered office. She held her hand out. I shyly grasped her hand and shook it.

"Well, we have a form here that you can fill out," she said.

"Okay," I replied.

She went to a big grey filing cabinet and shuffled some papers. After a couple of seconds, she pulled out a form, and grabbed a pen from the desk behind her. As she handed it to me, she said, "you can sit at this table and fill this out."

I looked at the small round table beside me and sat rather awkwardly down on the hard, plastic chair that was drawn up to it. Sitting at the very edge of the chair, and with my hands shaking, I quietly and quickly filled out the form.

When I handed over the form, Lorie thanked me and said she would be in touch. I walked out the door and down the steps back to the front reception where Darlene was waiting. As we walked out the door together, Darlene said, "Way to go! You did it."

I smiled, but the fear of doing something new made me shiver inside. It wasn't long before I heard back from Lorie and began volunteering at the Native Canadian Centre on a regular basis. It gave me life, something to look forward to each day, and taught me many things. It taught me people skills, office skills, and how to do event planning. I made friends and finally began learning about my culture and traditions. This is also where I learned about community and where I met my very dear friend C.A. He was a friend who became a very important part of my life and was someone who despite his own struggles always encouraged me and supported me in everything I did.

While I was at the Native Centre I began what I had always wanted to do—write for a community newsletter. Through the History Program Coordinator and then Editor of the Native Canadian newsletter, Monica, I began my column "Life's Journey." The column chronicled the ups and downs in my life. Though I had a couple of pieces of poetry published elsewhere, starting my column was the official launch of my professional writing career. It wasn't long after I started my column that I began contributing articles to other First Nations news outlets. Volunteering and being around the people at the Friendship Centre gave me the confidence to try new things.

I also learned important life lessons. One of these lessons was how to cope with the death of someone close to me. When my dear friend C.A. passed away, I began to appreciate the small things. I began to learn that even when someone close to you passes, they are still around, but in ways you can't necessarily see.

During my time with C.A., I had learned that I couldn't cut myself off from experiencing new adventures. He had encouraged me to go after what I wanted. C.A.'s life was cut short, and I realized that he hadn't been given the chance to pursue what he wanted to its fullest, and out of my love for him, I needed to do this for myself. I finally took the time to discuss the idea of going back to school for a post-secondary education with my social worker Darlene.

The day I walked into First Nations House at the University of Toronto was a day I'll never forget. Darlene and I walked into the Academic Support worker's office.

"What programs are available for Christine to come back to school?" Darlene asked the woman at the desk.

The woman's name was Tracey King. I sat across from her as she sat at her desk explaining the difference between the two programs that I could apply to in order to get into undergraduate studies. I remember the laughter and joking that was going on outside her office and how it made me feel at ease. Tracey's smile lit up the room as she explained the steps I could take to get into the University of Toronto.

"There is the Transitional Year Program (TYP) that will give you the necessary experience to get into your undergrad program or there is the Academic Bridging Program—it is available for those who already have some post secondary experience," she explained.

After a few minutes of back-and-forth conversation and setting up a subsequent appointment, I applied for the Academic Bridging Program. I began my undergraduate studies in the Academic Bridging Program at the University of Toronto in 2004. I had wanted to go back to school but had been too scared to do anything about it. I feared that I couldn't apply myself and excel at it. Voices from my past bounced around my head telling me, "You'll never be anything, or amount to anything."

When I was accepted into the Academic Bridging Program, I almost had to pinch myself because I couldn't believe that my dream of going back to school was coming true at last. I signed up for the Intro to English Literature course. I remember the trepidation I felt at walking down St. George Street, looking for the building where my class would be held. Darlene walked me to my class that day.

"I had tears in my eyes as I walked away because I was so proud of you," she told me later.

****

The Academic Bridging Program was like nothing I had ever experienced before. I had chosen the English course because of my love for reading and writing, but I felt out of my element because so many years had passed since I had sat in a classroom. Here I was, an adult amongst twenty-year-olds, studying Shakespeare, Chaucer, Kafka, and learning how to dissect and analyze works I hadn't seen since my first attempt at college back in Windsor.

At this time in my life, I was very timid and socially anxious. I sat in the very back of the room because I didn't want to draw attention to myself. If my professor happened to call on me, my cheeks would turn red, and I would want the floor to swallow me up. Mind you, my professor was great, and I utilized office hours when I absolutely had to, but otherwise I kept to myself, and barely spoke to anyone else unless someone spoke to me first.

I managed to get through my Academic Bridging course, and a year later I enrolled in part time studies in the Arts and Science

Program. When I was accepted into the University of Toronto as a part time student in 2005, I knew I had finally shattered one stereotype that my adoptive parents had tried to instill in me: that First Nations women couldn't do anything.

I returned to school as a mature student and immersed myself into my studies. I started to learn about my people, their history, their struggles and their triumphs. I also learned to break away from the people who were hurting me. I finally freed myself from my adoptive father and his continuous emotional abuse. I learned to shape my own identity as an individual and, most importantly, as a grown woman.

After completing the Academic Bridging Program, I took my first class, "Introduction to Aboriginal Studies" with professor, Dr. Cynthia Wesley-Esquimaux.

One day I had to conjure up the nerve to speak to her. I shuffled to the front of the class, where Dr. Wesley-Esquimaux was standing and taking questions from the other students.

"What can I help you with?" she asked.

"Um... I just want to know how much is the class text going to cost?" I mumbled. I said it so quietly that she looked at me and asked me to look up and speak a little louder.

"I need to know how much the class text is going to cost," I repeated.

"That's much better!" she said. "I can hear you now! The text is going to be around ninety dollars and you can get it next week before class starts."

"Um, okay," I replied.

I turned around and made my way out of the room. My Intro to Aboriginal Studies course turned out to be one of my favorite classes in my first year of studies. I made a couple of friends in this class. I also learned the history of my people, the policies and acts that had come to govern my people, and the Indian Residential School System and its legacy of historical trauma. The course helped me to better understand the history of my own biological family. This encouraged me to work towards more change within my own life and myself.

During my second year of studies, I was introduced to First Nations House (FNH), a place that provides culturally relevant services to Indigenous students. FNH supports and unites academic success with personal growth and leadership development. First

Nations House offered many learning opportunities for me which included mentoring, friendship and support from staff like Jennifer Wesley, the receptionist, and the Resource Centre Coordinator Jackie Esquimaux-Hamlin. I was able to work with the Writer-in-Residence Cherie Dimaline and speak with traditional teacher Lee Maracle.

First Nations House gave me the opportunity to engage in work study positions. I was able to study abroad and spent five weeks in Sydney, Australia studying Indigenous Australia at the University of Sydney. I also traveled to Belize in Central America to learn about the Mayan people and their culture.

I never thought that I would ever get as comfortable as I did at First Nations House. When I walked in there, after one of my classes, I was so closed off from others that I couldn't carry on a conversation with anyone, no matter how hard they tried to get me to come out of my shell. Jennifer Wesley and I laugh about it today, but at the time I was extremely shy and introverted.

Jen told me how she remembers when I showed up at First Nations House. Huffing and puffing from climbing three flights of stairs, I walked into First Nations House with a stern look on my face, my shoulders hunched over, and a bandana wrapped tightly around my head. I wore the bandana because of an overzealous hairstylist who had decided that instead of straightening out my hair, she would give me a buzz cut instead. I didn't want anyone to see it.

"Hi, Welcome to First Nations House," Jen said with a big smile on her face.

"Um, hi, is Tracey King in?" I mumbled quietly.

"No, she's not in right now, but you can leave a message for her, if you'd like," Jen replied.

"Uh, no, that's okay," I said back and turned around and went back out the door.

I never thought about how I came across when I first went to First Nations House but today, we all laugh about it, because I have come so far from being that quiet, stern looking woman. First Nations House became a home away from home for me. I not only went there for classes, but I also went to their socials, Thanksgiving feasts, and workshops. I liked sitting and listening to lectures from visiting professors, Aboriginal Awareness week or the Indigenous Writer's Gathering, which was an enormously popular event.

First Nations House was very instrumental in helping me to see what I could do and what I could achieve. When I graduated in 2011, it was a dream come true. My degree represents so much more than just having a piece of paper in my hands, because there were so many times that I believed that I would not make it. My degree represents the struggle, the tears and the triumphs it took to get me to where I am today, and though it was scary to graduate, it was also exciting because I am the first in my biological family to obtain a university education. Getting my degree opened many doors for me. My education has allowed me to become a part of a community, learn my history in a deeper way and become engaged with like-minded people. I was able to find a job and gain the autonomy I had always sought. I strongly began to believe that if I worked hard enough for something I believe in, I can achieve it. Obtaining my degree gave me that confidence.

Master's degree graduation, University of Toronto, 2017.

With my Mom, Anna Smith (left).

THE DREAM

I'm asleep, wrapped in warm blankets. Shrill ringing jerks me awake and I throw off the blankets and grab my phone from the desk. I don't have my glasses on yet, so I squint at the unfamiliar number. My heart thumps.

"Hello?"

A female voice asks, "Is this Christine?"

"Yes…"

She clears her throat, "I'm sorry to inform you Christine, but your mother has passed away."

Here it is again. The dream. It comes often, invokes fear and rarely changes. I struggle to sit up and swing my legs over the edge of the bed. My feet touch the cold wooden floor as I reach for my glasses on the nightstand. I put them on and wipe the sweat from my brow. Slowly my eyes adjust to the dimness of my bedroom. My breathing is so erratic that I gulp like a fish yanked out of water. Chest heaving, heart thumping, I try to breathe through my nose. Inhale and exhale slowly. I shake my head, whispering into the empty room, "You'll be okay."

1… 2… 3…

Counting brings me back to the present and, in a moment of panic, calms my racing heart. Sometimes it works, sometimes it doesn't. I keep the tears from escaping. I don't want to feel like I have lost control.

The dream brings me back to the day I first met my mother. I had travelled three days on a Greyhound bus to meet her in Winnipeg, the halfway point between her home and mine. The repatriation worker had booked us a room at the St. Regis Hotel, and we were sitting in our room, marveling at the fact that we were finally together. There was an awkward silence between us. Each of us was uncertain of what to say. She was sitting on the edge of her bed eating an orange when she began to cough.

I was on the phone and at first, I didn't pay much attention to her coughing, but when the coughing continued and got worse, I hung up the phone.

"Are you okay?"

She nodded that she was.

But soon her whole body slid sideways, and she fell to the floor. Her face was an alarming shade of red and her legs and arms jerked. Oh God! My mother was choking! I ran over to where she lay, in between the wall and the side of her bed. Adrenaline was pumping through my body as I pried open her mouth and unclenched her teeth.

I reached in and dug out the fleshy piece of orange pulp that was blocking her airway. I tried to calm her as best I could. Then, someone began knocking loudly at our door.

BANG… BANG… BANG…

It sounded like a bull was trying to ram the door down. I ran over and swung it open. Two women stood there, obviously hotel guests who had overheard the commotion.

"What's going on? Is someone hurt?" one of the women asked.

The other one tried to look around me into the room. I couldn't talk yet, but I moved slightly to the side. Without another word, they strode past me. Then they saw my mother, still on the floor.

"I… I… don't know what happened," I told them. "One minute she was okay and the next, she was on the floor."

One of the women knelt down and peered into my mother's face. Then she told her friend, "Call the front desk right now!"

The second woman rushed to the phone on the nightstand and pressed 0.

I felt detached from everything going on around me. In the distance I heard, "We need an ambulance in room 204, hurry!"

I watch as the first woman brushed my mother's hair with her hand. "You're going to be okay… you're going to be okay." I'm taking in all of this, standing off to the side, frozen to the spot. Then there was a siren and an ambulance screeched to a halt outside the building. A moment later the elevator doors down the hall opened and I heard what sounded like a thousand feet stomping down the hallway. Two paramedics rushed in through the open door, a stretcher on wheels between them. They grabbed their medical supplies from the bags on top of the stretcher and one of them turned to me.

"What happened here?"

I could finally talk. "We were just sitting here. We just met a couple of hours ago, at the bus station. I was on the phone, and she was eating an orange." My nerves were making me ramble. "And I was talking, and then she was coughing. I asked her if she was okay, and she said she was. All of a sudden she started coughing harder and then she was on the floor. She was still coughing, and she turned red and her limbs were jerking." I bit down on my lip, trying to stop the flow of words, trying to be calm.

The paramedics leaned over my mother. One checked her pulse while the other tipped her head back and opened her mouth. He looked over at me. "How did you stop her from choking? There's nothing blocking her airway now."

"I opened her mouth and took out the pieces of orange she hadn't swallowed yet."

Everyone stared at me and the distance in the room dissipated. The silence was broken as the two paramedics nodded to each other. One said, "Good move." They lifted my mother onto the stretcher and maneuvered it back out into the hallway. Panic was rising in my throat like bile. I felt lightheaded and dizzy. The room began to spin. They'd wrapped her in a bright orange blanket and strapped an oxygen mask to her face, Her eyes were half closed. I grabbed onto the closest thing—a complete stranger, the woman who called the front desk—and whispered, *"Please be alright."* I followed the stretcher out of the room, down the elevator and into the ambulance.

The dream of my mother dying always brings me back to this memory. It is there when I close my eyes and its effects are always the same. The dream is something that I haven't been able to share adequately until now. It was inspired by the deep seated fear of losing my mom. I grew up not knowing who my mom was or what she looked like. I was always afraid that before I was able to meet her, it would be too late, and I would lose her all over again. Reconnecting with her has eliminated that fear; I know her, and just as important, she knows me. But now that we know each other that old fear has been replaced by a new one: that after finally meeting my mother, I will lose her again.

The dream reminds of this strange new fear.

In Ottawa at a 60s Scoop gathering after receiving a gift blanket.

A DIFFERENT WORLD

The gentle breeze wraps around me like a shawl here on the shores of Lake Simcoe.

Not a soul in sight.

Birds chirp on occasion, and two mallards float by. I am lost in thought.

Nothing disturbs me, not even the occasional car that drives by on the road above. I sit with my knees pulled up against my chest, my hands clasped around them. I'm hidden from the road by an expanse of grassy land. I don't feel the cold rocks on my backside or take note of the lapping water getting closer to my running shoes. Being here on a reserve brings to mind my ancestors. I live a life they could not begin to know. They did not know the sound of car horns honking, hear the incessant ringing of cellphones or have access to the kinds of solitude-breaking technology of today. They did not have to escape just to experience silence. There is no way they could have known that the world would become a place where people would lose respect for each other and the lands around them.

I wonder what my ancestors experienced. I want to learn what they knew so I can bring back tradition and culture. I want to speak Anishinaabemowin so that I can pass it down to the generations behind me. I want my niece to be proud to be half Anishinaabe and to pass it down to her own children.

Someone once told me that there was a time when Mother Earth was respected, a time when humans maintained relations with the whole natural world. We could step outside and not worry about breathing in toxins or chemicals. We could walk and appreciate the silence surrounding us. We didn't experience a constant cacophony of noise, see garbage lying around, worry about where we got our drinking water. If we went for a dip in the lake, we didn't see algae or have to worry about catching a disease. There were no chemicals choking the life out of our teeming rivers, streams and lakes.

I am an urban Indian. I have never known anything outside of city life. I did not grow up on my reserve, Peguis First Nation. What I knew of reserves was what I read in the newspapers or heard on the news and it was never good. In 2005 I picked up the local Indigenous newspaper "The Native Canadian" and read: "Kashechewan faces possible relocation from a land they know and have grown up on, due to flooding and contaminated water." I read about the high unemployment, the poverty, and the lack of suitable housing.

In my studies at the University of Toronto, I learned about the history of First Nations people and their communities. I learned how upheaval—separation from land, family and community—has a devastating impact both physically and psychologically, especially in a culture that holds great importance in connection with the land. Upheaval from land, family and community is all too familiar to many First Nations people.

Sitting on the rocks by the waters of Lake Simcoe, I think about the way of life that used to be and the worldview that has been re-introduced to me by this woman who was my first- and second-year professor but then became a mentor and a friend, Dr. Cynthia Wesley-Esquimaux. She brought me here to her First Nation on Georgina Island. It is a place that I can learn from and appreciate. She's gone out of her way to help me bridge the gap in my mind from city life to reserve life. She has gone out of her way to instill within me a knowledge I thirsted for all my life—to know who I am.

Since I first visited the Island five years ago, I've learned much more about family and community. I've listened to stories and have begun to understand the importance of Indigenous people having a voice and telling our stories. I have also learned that a home is a home wherever you make it. It can be wherever you want it to be—whether that is in the city or on the reserve. Your home can be made to reflect the worldview you believe in.

In Cynthia's home, the past intermingles with the present. It reflects her interest in bridging the gap between Indigenous heritage and the contemporary contributions we make today. It is in the artwork that adorns her walls and the library that is a book lover's dream to browse. When I stood on her deck, took in what was around me, and walked down to the waters not far from her house, I felt transformed. It is easy to look at the lake and see the changes that have happened in it. Where it once was clear, it is murky. You cannot help but wonder what the future holds for such a beautiful place, when there is such change happening everywhere.

Cynthia is a strong Indigenous woman who has experienced her own hardships. As an adult she went back to school and received her doctorate in Anthropology. She became involved in many committees and councils and had a work ethic that made her a role model to many people. Cynthia became my mentor and friend because she took the time to let me know that I could become a strong Anishinaabe Kwe too.

It is through such influential First Nations women that I am learning to rebound from negative experiences and awaken a social and cultural resiliency that I never thought was in me before. I have learned much from my first visit to Georgina Island. I have learned to scale the wall of personal, community and national resistance by learning to open my eyes and see that within I have a voice that needs to be heard.

It's time for me to head back to the mainland. I know my ride is waiting. I stand up reluctantly from my perch on the rocks at the edge of the lake. I brush myself off and pull my jacket closed. I am heading back to Toronto, but before I do; I pull out my camera to capture the stillness that surrounds me.

After, I take some tobacco out of a cigarette from my pack that is sitting beside me, I sprinkle it on the waters stretching out before me. I watch the current carry it into the lake and say "Chi miigwetch" for what I have learned, and what I have seen. I turn to walk away, but I am not sad. I know that I will be back. The wind dies down, but the shawl stays wrapped around my shoulders as I return to my home in the city.

THE ARTIST

I sit on the cold hard floor of my apartment, a blank canvas in front of me. I have a paintbrush clutched in my hand, and it's dipped in acrylic blue. There's silence all around me; I lean over and begin to paint. My hand moves as if it has a mind of its own, nothing distracts me, as shapes and colours materialize in front of me. A stroke here: and a stroke there… Lo and behold, a bear appears in front of me.

I've always been creative in one form or another. Whether it was writing in one of my many notebooks or drawing on whatever scraps of paper I could find, being creative has always calmed and grounded me, especially throughout my toughest times. For years though, I allowed my creativity to lay dormant within me. I listened to the words of unsupportive people in my past who told me I was "living in a dream world" thinking that I could be a writer and "get anywhere in life."

Throughout my early years, I let these insults burrow deep into my consciousness. One of my earliest memories of my burgeoning creativity happened when I was a child and I was locked inside my bedroom. I was constantly lonely so my sister would keep me company by sitting on the other side of my door and talking to me. Sometimes she would slide some paper and a couple of crayons under my bedroom door, and I would write or draw on the paper she gave me.

After finishing with the paper, I would slide the crumpled-up pieces of paper under the door to my sister who was waiting on the other side. It always felt good when I saw my sister's hand grab the piece of paper and heard her little voice say, "That's good, Christine!"

My sister encouraged me with those words of kindness at a time when no one else in my family would. In elementary school, a few of my teachers stood out because they encouraged and supported me. As I would walk beside them on yard duty during recess, they would encourage me to do the best I could. They would tell me I had great penmanship and I would be gently teased for always wanting my writing to look perfect. I always linked that with my love for writing.

In high school my Art and English teachers began to encourage me. They would take me aside and tell me, "Christine, we see a lot of potential in you." I carried those words around with me and held them close. They told me to be as creative as I wanted and to follow my dream of becoming a writer. I began to take a special interest in writing and drawing. Art and English became my favourite classes because I knew I could go into these classes and my teachers would encourage me in whatever I did. I would walk into my Art and English classes and get totally caught up in what I was being taught. I remember the pride I felt when the teacher would take my work and use it as an example for the others in my class. I wasn't afraid to read outside of what we were studying in class either. In fact, my teachers encouraged it, and more often than not, if you saw me walking down the street to and from school, I would have a book in my hand.

My early writing career began when I enrolled in a Journalism-Print Program at a college in my hometown of Windsor. Though I loved learning how to write news articles, and learning photography, I couldn't give the course my full attention because of illness. My college career ended when one day I was in the darkroom of my photography class, and I passed out in the middle of my teacher's talk on how to properly develop film.

After leaving college, I was in and out of the hospital but I began to think of my writing more seriously. Despite my trepidation, I submitted my first poem to a journal for publication. I was so excited when I learned that it had been accepted. The poem was aptly titled "The Past," and it ran in the Ontario Children's Aid Society Journal. Sometime after that, the Director of the Children's Aid Society was driving me home one day following my appointment with my social worker.

"Your poem makes it sound as if you really had a terrible time with your adoptive parents," he said. "But they took you in."

Despite this pushback to writing about my experiences, I continued to write. I filled notebook after notebook with my various writings and sent out poems to various small print publications such as *Pen and Ink Magazine* in Ann Arbor Michigan and the *Roman Catholic Children's Aid Journal*. I also sent some poems to poetry.com which turned out to be a kind of vanity press. Sometimes, I learned the hard way about being a writer and getting published—but I learned.

In 2006 while volunteering at the Native Canadian Centre of Toronto I began writing my column, "Life's Journey," for the Native Canadian newsletter. In the column I began to chronicle my life experiences and healing journey and covered events at the Centre and other places around the Toronto community. Around this time, a fellow classmate at U of T who was the editor of The Window, a small newspaper based out of New College, approached me and asked me to write book reviews of Indigenous writers.

I also started writing for *FNH Magazine*, a magazine based out of First Nations House at the University of Toronto and as my confidence grew, I branched out further. I sent a letter of introduction and writing samples to *Anishinabek News*, wrote a few articles for the *Native Journal*, started my own blog, wrote book reviews for *Windspeaker*, submitted short stories to places like *Growing Up Girl: Voices from Marginalized Spaces* and creative Indigenous journals like *Yellow Medicine Review* where two of my creative non-fiction pieces were published. I then started writing for *New Tribe Magazine*.

BANFF

In 2011, after encouragement from the then Writer In Residence at First Nations House at the University of Toronto, I met one of my writing mentors, Cherie Dimaline. Dimaline is an acclaimed Metis author who has published several fiction books. Her most popular book is the award-winning novel, *The Marrow Thieves.*

After receiving encouragement from Cherie, I applied for my first writing grant from the Canada Council for the Arts. The application was for an Aboriginal Emerging Writers Grant. Successful applicants were provided with a two-week residency at the Banff Centre for the Arts to work on a manuscript while being mentored by a faculty of established writers. The residency was followed by ten weeks of online mentoring with one of the mentors from the Banff program to hone and polish your manuscript.

The purpose of the Aboriginal Emerging Writer program is to encourage the artistic and creative development of emerging Indigenous writers and storytellers in a supportive, artistic and cultural environment. It is an opportunity for writers to develop their writing and storytelling amongst other emerging Indigenous writers. Being chosen as one of eight 2011 recipients of the Aboriginal Emerging Writer grant was a life-changing experience that helped my writing career reach new heights.

As a freelance journalist, it has always been a dream of mine to expand my writing repertoire. The Banff program gave me a unique opportunity to study with other accomplished emerging writers and established authors such as Anishinaabe writer and owner of Kegedonce Press, Kateri Akiwenzie-Damm, Métis poet Gregory Scofield, Indigenous Australian author Bruce Pascoe, and the acclaimed and prolific Salish writer Lee Maracle.

Being in Banff was amazing. The scenery is breathtakingly beautiful. To get to where we spent our time amongst our peers and the faculty members who taught us how to edit and revise our writing, was a pathway that made me feel like I had been transported to a mystical place. Walking to the cottage, where we studied and learned, I made my way down a pathway with a small bridge, and if I was alert enough at 9 a.m., I could see elk grazing on the grass around me. The backdrop to all of this were the tall and majestic mountains.

The two-week residency at the Banff Centre was like boot camp, but it was a boot camp that focused on what I loved to do—writing! We were taught various techniques to overcome writer's block and various types of writing, including humour writing. One of my favorite stories was written during a writing exercise at Banff. It's a short story titled "A Step by Step Guide to Annoying Your Teenage Daughter" (see Appendix). I remember sitting in a circle with my fellow writers, and our program advisors giving us the assignment of writing something that required following steps. As I sat there, pondering what the heck I could write about, my advisor, Kateri Akiwenzie-Damm came up to me. I don't remember the other step-by-step assignments she suggested to me, but as soon as I as heard about the one about annoying your teenage daughter, I jumped on it and furiously began to write. It was the first time that I had tried my hand at humour writing.

I read the story during our reading night. It was open to the general public and though I was as nervous as heck, the laughter afterwards buoyed my spirits. Being part of the Emerging Writer Residency Program was the best thing that could have happened to me. Since participating in that program, I have submitted other pieces of work to various places and I won a grant from the Ontario Arts Council to continue my writing project. The program gave me the confidence to try other creative outlets.

Creativity has always been a part of my life, but it needed to be awakened. Today, I sit on the cold hard floor of my apartment, a blank canvas in front of me. A few short steps away lies an open book with a pen beside it. I no longer feel the need to choose because I can do either. The artist in me is no longer hidden or afraid and I can now confidently say, "I'm a writer, a visual artist and a photographer." I feel free to express myself the way I want to now.

WINNIPEG

Travelling is in my blood. If I don't pick up and go at least once a year, I get antsy. It didn't used to be like that, but when I started travelling a few years ago, I realized how much I like it. There is something about packing a suitcase, standing in line at the airport, going through check-in, settling into your seat on the airplane, and taking off to a new destination that makes me smile.

This time I wasn't heading to a warm destination like California or Belize or to Alberta to learn from other writers at the Banff Centre. This time, I was going on one of the most memorable trips of my life: I was travelling to Winnipeg to see my mom. It was late October, not the greatest time to head to the place everyone calls "Winterpeg," but my flight was booked, and I was raring to go. My mom had sent me some cash from monies she had just received from the government for her residential school settlement so that I could get myself an airline ticket.

I hadn't seen her in ten years, and I wasn't sure what to expect this time around. She had only just started contacting me a few months before we decided that I would go out to see her again at her new place in Ashern, Manitoba. Ashern is a sleepy little hamlet of about 1,500 people. It's an hour drive north from Peguis First Nation, my home reserve. I call this town sleepy because there is literally no action in the town at all—unless you witnessed the antics of my mom's partner, Jim.

"You're way too serious, you need to relax," he told me.

From then on, he was always joking around or playing pranks to get a rise out of me. He'd bang on the back door, wait for me to open the door, and then yell "BOO!" The more annoyed I was, the more he'd laugh.

Hanging out at the Resource Centre was another social highlight in Ashern. My mom and Jim would go there every day to have coffee and shoot the breeze with other older people in the town. It was a happy place but the most action you got was people laughing and joking or singing snippets of songs.

This was my second time travelling to see my mom. The first visit had been over ten years earlier when a repatriation worker organized a reunion between my mom and I and we had stayed at the infamous Regis Hotel in downtown Winnipeg. This time, I didn't take the bus or spend three days getting there. It was a two-hour airplane flight. My friend Jackie had helped me book the flight through WestJet airlines, and I arranged with my friend Verne to pick me up at my apartment and drive me to the airport.

Arriving at the airport was uneventful but walking through security screening was a bit embarrassing especially when I accidently left my belt on my jeans and set the alarm off.

"Ma'am please step back," the airport security officer said. "Remove your belt and come through again."

Embarrassing! My heart started racing and my face turned about fifty shades of red. The line up behind me grew as I fumbled to remove my belt. I was flustered and sweating as I walked through the screening again. *Please,* I thought, *let me get through this without setting off that damn alarm again.*

Success! I passed through security, gathered all my carry-on items, and hobbled over to a nearby chair to put my shoes and belt back on before heading to the gate. Thankfully, I boarded the plane without incident. I had a window seat on the flight to Winnipeg, which I totally loved. I could look out the window at the clouds, and I didn't have to worry about other passengers or the air flight attendants brushing against me as they walked up and down the aisles.

As the airplane took off, I grabbed onto the arms of my seat, feeling my eardrums pop as the cabin pressure changed. As I looked out my window, I saw a shining orb that seemed to follow the plane the whole way to my destination. It disappeared as I disembarked from the plane. I felt truly blessed and wondered if it was my ancestors showing me they were happy that I was heading back home.

The city of Winnipeg felt so strange to me. I didn't know what to expect of Winnipeg, because people had always told me, "Winnipeg is pretty rough—you have to be careful." I had seen newspaper accounts of crime in downtown Winnipeg and read about the racism towards Native people. I was a bit afraid knowing that I had to hang around the city until I could catch a bus to Ashern. I didn't know what the heck I was going to do. The only money I had was in my wallet—a couple of twenties, maybe a ten-dollar bill, and a coin or two rattling around in my change purse.

I retrieved my baggage and went down a set of escalators, pulling my overloaded suitcase behind me. I headed to the nearest exit so that I could have a much-needed cigarette. *Ah! Winter, you gotta love it*, I thought as the revolving doors opened to a below-freezing wind that hit me smack dab in the face.

After drawing a few puffs from my cigarette and smashing what was left of it under my heel, I gathered up the courage to go over to a valet waiting outside his car at the arrivals door to ask for directions.

"Excuse me, sir, how do I get to the Greyhound bus station?" I asked.

The man's face lit up, and his hands moved animatedly as he spoke. "Just cross this street," he said. "Go through the underground parking lot, and the station is right there."

"Thank you, sir!" I said and started my trek.

My back started aching from carrying my heavy bags, and my non-existent Nish butt hurt from sitting on the plane, even though two hours wasn't that long. Ten minutes later, I arrived at the Winnipeg Greyhound station, and make my way to the counter.

"Hello, I need a one-way ticket for Ashern," I said.

"Oh, that bus isn't until 9:30 p.m.," the Greyhound attendant said as he continued typing and looking at his computer screen.

"You've got to be kidding me!"

"Nope," he said. "The bus schedule has been like this for years, but at least you'll get a lot of shopping in!"

I purchased my bus ticket and stuffed the paper into my purse. I looked over at the lockers.

"You can store your suitcase there in the lockers," he said. "It will cost you five or six dollars more, otherwise you'll have to carry your suitcase with you."

Thinking; *Heck no!* I made my way over to the lockers. There were big lockers, the size of a kitchen cupboard, and little lockers. As I stood in front of locker 125, the maintenance man saw my confusion about which locker to use and came over to where I was standing.

"Take a small locker and put five dollars in so that you can have the maximum number of hours before your bus comes," he advised me.

I opened the locker door, and started to put my suitcase in.

"Where are you from?" the maintenance guy asks me.

"Toronto," I told him. "Do you know how I can get downtown? My bus doesn't come until later tonight."

After he told me which bus to take, I walked away feeling thankful for the kindness this stranger had shown me. I walked outside and crossed the small parking lot to the bus stop. I'm alone. I hope I make it downtown all right; I thought to myself.

The bus trip should have been easy, but because I was anxious being somewhere new, I made it more difficult and got myself lost. I was supposed to take the number 15 bus and get off at Main and Portage. The bus driver was anything but helpful or kind.

"Where is the nearest shopping mall?" I asked him when I got on the bus.

"There are a ton of malls in this city," he said. "Just sit down."

My heart was beating like crazy. I sat down and I hung onto my purse and backpack as tightly as I could. As I traveled all around the city, I took in the sights around me: dilapidated buildings, newer buildings that all seemed to be government buildings.

Interesting architecture, and interesting people, I thought.

After what seemed like two hours, the bus driver finally noticed that I had stayed on his bus for the whole route. He turned around in his seat and motioned with his hand for me to go up and see him.

"Ma'am, where did you want to go? You've been on here for a long time," he said.

"Sir," I mumbled, "I've never been here before and I don't know where Main and Portage is, or where I can go until my bus comes tonight. Someone told me there were shopping malls that I can go to, but I don't know where they are."

"Well, we passed Main and Portage a long, long time ago!" he said. "When you hear the system say CITY HALL, come up to me and I'll tell you where you need to get off."

The bus seemed like it was in the middle of nowhere. Houses were few and far between and the landscape was dotted with industrial buildings. The bus lurched along for a few minutes with me as the lone passenger. Finally, I heard the screech of the brakes and a few people straggled on.

From my seat at the front of the bus, I noticed that almost all the passengers were Native like me. A couple of them were pushing baby strollers, the children inside them staring out with big brown eyes. *I'm surrounded by other Anishinaabek*, I thought, and I laughed to myself as I took in the way that they were dressed, and heard the slow drawl in their voices, followed by the inflection *"eh"* after each sentence.

I overheard a conversation between a thin white woman and an older Native man.

"Hey, how are ya?" the lady said as her eyes met the Native man's eyes across the aisle.

"Oh, I'm good, eh," he replied.

"I haven't seen you in forever," she said back. "Where ya been?"

"Oh, I was in Halifax, eh," the guy said. A big smile spread across his face, as his hand patted the battered old suitcase on the floor beside him. "I just welcomed my latest grandkid."

"Oh wow," said the lady, nodding her head.

There was silence for a couple of seconds and then the conversation shifted to her old man and how he ended up on probation instead of having to serve three years in the slammer.

I shook my head at this conversation because it's not something I would want to be talking about, especially on a bus full of people. I realized though that conversations on the TTC in Toronto are no different than the buses here in Winnipeg.

Through the chatter of everyone on the bus, an automated voice broke through.

"CITY HALL!" it announced.

I got up off my seat and wrangled my way around the two baby strollers to stand at the bus driver's elbow.

"Okay sir, where do I get off, is it here?"

"No," he said. "Stay right here and I'll tell you in a minute."

As I hung onto a bar near the bus driver's shoulder, the bus seemed to speed up, or maybe it was my wishful thinking. Seconds later, the bus came to a halt. The driver turned to me.

"At the lights behind me, cross over where the RBC building is," he said. "Go down the steps and there's Winnipeg Square..."

"Thank you, sir," I replied as I squeezed between two people who were trying to get on the bus.

My feet hit the sidewalk and I heard the screeching sound of the bus door closing. The bus left a cloud of dust in its wake, as it sped off.

I am alone... I thought to myself, as I turned and made my way across the street. Unfamiliar sounds, sights and smells were all around me. I was on a new journey.

****

Winnipeg Square is a mall located off the corner of Main Street and Portage Street in downtown Winnipeg. This is where I ended up after disembarking at the City Hall bus stop.

I realized after hopping off the bus and looking like a lost soul in the middle of a busy sidewalk that there's only so much you can do when you are becoming acquainted with a little part of a block in a strange city. I could either look like a tourist or I could walk with purpose and let others around me know, "hey, I belong here, just like you!"

For a second, I hesitated, but then I lit a cigarette, and inhaled deeply, my lungs and chest contracting as I breathed in and breathed out. I let out a huge sigh… "AH!" as a little cloud of smoke escaped my mouth. The nicotine calmed my nerves almost immediately, or at least I'd like to think it did. Seasoned professionals would tell me otherwise. I could almost hear the words of my therapist in my head. "Come on, Christine," she'd say to me. "You know cigarettes aren't good for you. You should quit."

"Ah," I'd say indignantly, "but it's something I need. I'm not going to quit." even though I knew better.

I cast that thought from my head and turned to walk to the corner. I felt like I was invisible. I could have been a ghost or a spirit to the people walking by me. They were either staring at the ground or looking through me as though there was no substance to me at all. I was just another tourist as far as anyone could guess, in this city far from home.

Crossing the street, I noticed the RBC sign that the bus driver told me to look for. I walked down the sidewalk, brushing past some suits. You know, those people all dressed to the nines who carry briefcases, hurrying to their all-important 9–5 jobs in swanky government offices (*oh, how I wish I could be one of them!*). There were a couple of police officers in the crowd to boot.

I saw some doors and walked down the steps, careful not to slip on the thin ice that I saw forming in this bitterly cold weather. As the doors swung open, immediately to my right were a couple of boutiques, a restaurant, a pub, and a food court. The mixtures of the different foods being cooked assaulted my nose. Ah! There's nothing like the smell of overcooked rice, pizza, burgers and fries all in one sniff.

To escape the smells of the food court, I ducked into a store and looked around. My eyes adjusted to the dim lighting in the store. I noticed some jewelry, and honed in on what I saw as Native-themed rings. I picked up a ring that had a bear paw engraved in it. I turned it around and around in my hand, as I contemplated whether to buy it. I walked around the store, with this ring in my hand and looked at everything from T-shirts that said Winnipeg on them, to hand towels and Inukshuks. I finally decided, I could do without the ring and put it back. I walked out of the store two minutes later and walked back to the stairs leading to the great outdoors.

Walking back up the steps, I decided that I'd go exploring. I knew that I was not going to go very far. It was a hassle just trying to get to Winnipeg Square, and I didn't want to get lost again. I pulled my jacket close and started walking. As I made my way down the sidewalk, I started seeing the stores that surrounded me—a mom and pop convenience store, a TD Bank, a pawnshop or two, with signs that yell "COME ON IN, WE'LL TAKE YOUR GOLD." I passed a crowd of people waiting at a bus stop then I saw a News store.

Ducking out of the cold, I popped into the News store. At the front of the store was the magazine section, and further back I saw an 18-and-over section. I turned and headed directly for the magazine section. I was in heaven—all my favorite writing magazines were there at my fingertips. I started leafing through them one by one. As I was standing there, out of the corner of my eyes I saw a Writer's Digest magazine. I figured if I was going to be spending the day in the city, I might as well buy something that would keep me occupied. There's nothing like reading! I picked up the magazine then walked around the store one more time just to see if there was anything else that would grab my attention. Nothing did so I walked up to the cashier and made my purchase.

Cutting in front of me was a lady with her Lotto 6/49 ticket. I wanted to say, "Hey, I was here first!" but I stayed silent. I should have said something, but I didn't want to cause a scene. After handing my cash to the store clerk, I walked out. Back out on the sidewalk and wondering what the heck to do next, I glanced across the street and saw another one of my favorite stores—a dollar store.

You've gotta love the dollar stores that dot big Canadian cities, and the cheap bargains they offer. After crossing the street one more time, I go into the dollar store and start walking the aisles. I picked up a pair of fingerless gloves and saw a giant Tootsie Roll that I would have loved to sink my teeth into but the glare of the fluorescent lights and someone who seemed to be trailing me made me put everything down and leave the store. I headed back to Winnipeg Square.

Once inside, I went to the ATM. I checked my bank balance and saw that I could only take out six dollars. Boy, did I ever feel Nish, going in and saying to the bank teller "Hi, can I take out six dollars?" I was almost laughing when the bank teller looked up at me.

"Would you like a five-dollar bill and a loonie?" she said.

I wanted to tell her, "Oh no, I'd like it all in change," but I didn't. For some reason, I didn't think she would find my comment very funny.

At the food court I decided to have my usual, chicken fried rice. The food wasn't great—it seemed dry to my palate—but it was something and I hadn't eaten since my snack on the airplane.

While sitting in the food court, I texted my friend Michelle, who lived an hour away in Beausejour, Manitoba. She texted me back and said she would meet me. After gulping my food down, I got up and started walking around Winnipeg Square again. A little over an hour and a half later, while making what seemed like my fiftieth lap around the little boutiques in Winnipeg Square, Michelle finally arrived.

Michelle and I had met back in 2006 when we both attended the Banff Emerging Writer's Residency. Seeing a familiar face while in Winnipeg was a great relief, and when I looked up from my magazine and saw her approaching me, I smiled because I knew she didn't have to come to meet me.

For a couple of seconds we stood in front of each other, silent, but then we began to talk like no time had passed between us at all. She asked me where I wanted to go, and I replied, "Oh, I don't know."

"Ok," she replied. "I know some places. Let's go!"

We trekked over to the parking garage where Michelle had parked her car. We hopped into her car and after driving out of the murkily-lit garage, Michelle turned to me.

"Hey, I can take you to the Forks. I think you'd like that."

"Sure, sounds great," I said.

And off we went.

After a fun afternoon catching up with Michelle, she dropped me off at the bus station for the two hour bus trip to see my mom.

****

I arrive at my mom's around midnight after a two-hour bus ride.

The old brown worn-out couch had seen better days, but this is where I sleep while here at my mom's. Every night, as the sun starts to set, and my mom and her partner have gone off to sleep, I methodically pull the cushions off the couch, and stack them in the corner by the front door. Yes, I am sleeping in the front room, but I don't mind. After all, it's somewhere to sleep, and I know I'm not alone—my mom and her partner are around the corner in their bedroom if I need them.

I'll let you in on a secret, I'd rather sleep in the front room than retire to the basement. Even after all these years, I'm still afraid of basements and the deep dark secrets that can hide around the murky corners. Yes, I'm a grown woman, but my fears of the dark and of what can hide in basements still scare me. I don't know if I will ever be able to let go of that.

As I start to doze off each night, I feel a presence. I try to ignore it, but when it first happens it scares me. I toss and turn on the thin mattress, trying to find a comfortable position to sleep in. As I am lying there, all of a sudden, the mattress moves, as though something or someone is lightly bouncing onto the bed at my feet. My heart quickens and my breath catches in my throat.

The first night it happens, I jump up and put my glasses on to see what is going on. Their cat, Rusty, is nowhere to be seen, nor is their dog Duffy. The next night it happens and I try to lay as still as I can, in my head willing it silently to go away. This presence makes itself known every night as I am about to drop off to sleep. At first it makes me uneasy, but then I slowly grow used to it. I come to expect the bounce of the spirits' feet onto my mattress because it lasts only mere seconds. Sometimes I wonder, "what is this presence, what does it want?" Then I remember a teaching from a long time ago—spirits usually don't mean any harm, they're here for one reason or another, and all I have to do is put some tobacco down if I really want to know why. I tell myself, *Nothing is going to hurt you, it's time to get some sleep.* My eyes close, and soon I am off in dreamland.

****

Ashern, Manitoba is a little town in the middle of the prairie. The houses are sparse and placed far apart. In every direction the flat prairie landscape seems vast and unchanging. For a city girl like me, it feels cold and uninviting. This land, though, is what my mom and her partner call home, and every morning that I am there, I awake to the sound of the winds around the house, the rattling of the chain they use to put Duffy their dog on outside, and Jim yelling, "Heeellloooo Canada!" as he opens the door to let the dog out and check the day's weather.

My mom and Jim sit down at the kitchen table, and I groggily make my way over to the table to sit with them. It's early, the pink of the new day still present in the frosted windowpane above the sink. My mom gets up from her chair and ambles over to the kitchen counter. She's pulling out mugs from the cupboard. She's making her morning tea, while Jim has his morning coffee and smoke. They don't have a coffee machine, like the Tassimo system I use back home. They use a worn-out kettle that my mom picked up from their local Goodwill, the kind that whistles and makes you cringe and want to throw it across the room because the whistle is so shrill. Jim lights up a cigarette, and the smell of it makes me reach for mine.

We sit there, shooting the breeze, drinking our coffee and tea, and an hour or so passes. I look outside, and then glance at the clock. It's 9:00 a.m.

"We're going to go to the Centre," my mom and Jim tell me. "But you can stay here and sleep some more if you want. You can meet us afterwards."

I nod my head, and head back to the couch. I'm still tired, but I can't sleep now. I figure I will do some reading. A few of the books I have brought with me on this trip are sitting on the coffee table. I climb under the thin blanket that adorns my bed and grab a book. As I am reading, I drop off back to sleep. When I awake an hour later, the house is quiet. I sit in the silence of the house for a few minutes, and then decide I had better get showered and out the door to meet my mom and Jim. I grab the handle at the end of the mattress and pull it up. The only sound is the metal hitting the couch as I fold the bed back into its hiding place in the couch. I put the cushions back into place and drag the coffee table back in front of the couch.

I kneel down at my suitcase and think about what I'm going to wear. I pull out a pair of jeans out and a T-shirt. I've decided on my favorite black jeans and a T-shirt that has a buffalo emblazoned across its front. Lastly, I grab my hoodie and place the outfit on the couch. I walk to the washroom, prepare the shower and hop in. Minutes later, all dressed and ready to go, I look around the house one last time, and then go down the rickety wood stairwell to the backdoor.

As I pull the door open, the cold air blasts me in the face. *I'm awake now!* I think as I pull my jacket close. Securely shutting the back door behind me, I set out for what my mom and Jim call "downtown."

There is no cell phone service here in Ashern, at least for me because of the phone plan I have, but by habit, I bring my iPhone and turn my tunes on. Music blares through the little buds into my ears, and I smile as I start my trek. I navigate my way from the back door of my mom's house, around the long chain link fence surrounding their property, and down a barren path. My boots crunch through the snow, leaving their mark on the cold hard ground. I'm greeted by the barking of two dogs along the way. No other soul is in sight.

It's so different from the city life I am used to in Toronto, where people seldom walk slowly, and are always on the go. A big whoosh of air leaves my lips, and I see my breath before me. It's cold in Toronto, but it didn't prepare me for the intense cold here. I hadn't expected Ashern to be as cold as it is.

My pace quickens as the wind whips around me. Small buildings dot this town's landscape, but they are few and far between. Through squinted eyes, I see the Ashern community hall, and kitty corner to that, is the town's motel, a dilapidated building that I find out is home to a few displaced First Nations people who have had to evacuate their reserve due to flooding. Though there are street signs, they're a little hard to read. I see Manitoba written on the signs with the little buffalo emblem below. I am excited by this because I know *mashkaadebishke* is my totem.

Here in Ashern, I find that I don't have to rush against a crowd of people just to cross the street, and I take my time revelling in the quiet that surrounds me. I see a small, weathered building on my right, with a sign above the door that says "Ashern Support Centre." I know my mom and Jim are there because I see his little tractor with the ski-doo trailer behind it. It is parked on an angle on the empty street corner.

I pull the door open. Standing in the doorway for a second, my eyes adjust from the harsh sunlight to the dim indoor light. I glance around the room. A worn-out couch sits to my left, alongside hangers of old clothing hanging haphazardly. I see boxes of books, an occasional knick-knack, and the old computer desk to the far left that holds a desktop PC and printer. A lady is sitting at the desk, hunched over, with her back towards me.

After taking everything in, my eyes are drawn back to the long worn-out plastic utility table. I see my mom and Jim sitting there. Jim startles me when he says in his booming voice, "Hey you made it!"

I take off my earphones and smile. I walk over and sit down at the end of the table. People wonder who I am.

"This is my daughter," she says. "She came from Toronto to visit."

"Oh!" says a lady sitting at the other end of the table. "What's your name?"

"Christine," I mumble.

There's chatter for a few seconds.

"You look so much like your mom," a few people comment.

The bantering back and forth continues. I look at everyone and sit down. Everyone starts laughing.

"We should call you Little Banana," they say, "because your mom's nickname is Big Banana!"

Everyone is sitting and drinking coffee and tea. I sit quietly for five or ten minutes before my mom gets up.

"Come on," she says.

"Where are we going?" I ask, as I follow my mom out the door.

"I'm going to show you around," my mom replies.

We start to walk this sleepy little town's streets. There's a Sears outlet store that we walk around in for a few minutes. Then we check out a couple of gift shops. Our last stop is the Goodwill. Here, my mom seems to have the most fun. She's going up and down the aisles, checking out the secondhand shoes, electric kettles, and other items.

I notice a bin of stuffed animals, and busy myself looking through them. I see a few plastic dolls, the kind I would have loved as a kid, but find almost freakish now. I see a huge white bear, and out of the corner of my eye, I see my mom looking over at me, She heads over to where I'm standing.

"I love bears! This one is so cute!" It didn't matter that the bear was huge, I fell in love with it. My mom looks at the bear and grabs it out of my hands. She starts to walk to the front of the store to the cashier. It's the first stuffed animal I ever received from my mom, and after we walk out of the Goodwill store I'm hanging onto it like crazy. My mom tells me there's not much else to check out. And I must agree. There are about as many stores on the main street of Ashern as there are on half a block back in Toronto. Two minutes later, we walk back to the Ashern Support Centre, and I am holding the big bear as we walk towards the door to head back inside.

Jim is sitting outside on the bench, puffing away on a cigarette. With the cigarette smoke billowing around him, he grins and gets up. "Whatcha got there?" he drawls, as he takes a couple of puffs on his cigarette and then smooshes it under his foot on the sidewalk. He walks towards us, grabs our packages and strides toward his tractor. He puts everything down in the rickety trailer he has set up behind his tractor.

"You ready to get going?" he asks.

We both nod our heads. My mom climbs onto the skidoo seat that's strapped to the trailer behind Jim's tractor. I sit down on the trailer's floor behind her, bracing myself for the ride ahead. My hands are holding on so hard to the sides of the trailer, I can feel the grain of the wood against my skin. I wonder if holding on so tight will leave a permanent scar on my hands or if I'll be bruised on my butt from the roughness of the wood against my characteristically flat Anishinaabe butt.

Jim hops onto the tractor. He looks back briefly, and I hear him turn the ignition. As the engine roars to life and we speed off, I shake my head and hang on for dear life. As we pick up speed, in my head, I am yelling *WHEEEEE!* I've never ridden in a trailer pulled behind a tractor before, let alone one going at breakneck speed. This is a first.

I can't wait to tell my friends back home.

With my niece Sam (right)

AN INEXPLICABLE BOND

I'm standing outside the entrance of the Greyhound bus station in downtown Toronto. My hand is at my brow, trying to shield the sun from my eyes because it's blocking my view of seeing where my niece Sam is sitting on the bus. For a couple of seconds, I can't see her, but then I catch a glimpse of her through the window waving almost timidly at me. I smile and wave back. I stand there because I want to make sure that she heads off safely. Minutes later, her bus pulls out of the station and I feel my heart leap into my throat. I start to walk away from the bus station, stopping momentarily to light up a cigarette. I take a drag on my cigarette, inhaling deeply. The smoke curls out of my mouth and into the stagnant air around me. I start to head towards the subway station, but then to distract myself from the sadness that is trying to overwhelm me, I walk to the World's Biggest Bookstore, about a block away from the bus station. The World's Biggest Bookstore was a mecca of books that somehow manages to soothe me whenever I am feeling a bit of sadness or distress.

I can't quite explain the sadness I feel. I am choked up because, after a week of Sam staying with me, it will be different being back in my apartment alone. I'm going to miss her even though I will see Sam in a couple of months at Thanksgiving or when I head to Windsor to spend Christmas with her and her two little sisters.

As I'm walking, I pull my iPhone from my jeans pocket and scroll my finger down my contact list. I see my niece's father's name pop up, and type him a quick text message while trying to balance my purse and diet Pepsi.

"She got on the bus okay, and she's heading home," I write.

Holding my phone in one hand, I continue my trek to the bookstore. The sidewalk isn't too busy but trying to cross the street is another story. I'm standing at the edge of the sidewalk, watching the cars whiz by me. As I'm about to step off the sidewalk, I almost lose my balance because in my haste to cross the street and get to the bookstore, I twist my ankle slightly. I wince as the pain shoots through my ankle and up my calf.

"Damn it!" I mutter to myself. I step back up onto the sidewalk, quickly reorient myself and try to cross the street again. Striding as fast as I can before the next car comes along, I feel my phone buzz in my jean pocket. My hand goes into my pocket, but I hold off on glancing at it until I'm across the street. Safely across the street, I pull my phone out and look down at the blurry screen. I chuckle at the text message I've received from my Sam's father, Dave.

"Okay, thanks, you can rest now."

I text back "lol" and then send another quick text: "text me to let me know that she got home okay?"

He texts, " ☺ No" and then another message quickly pops up, "Yeah, okay."

My phone goes silent, and I put it back into my pocket. I've reached the bookstore. I swipe a Kleenex across my forehead, pull at the door and walk in.

It was April 26, 1996, when I stood in the delivery room of the hospital and witnessed my niece being born. I stood to the side of my sister's bed and watched the doctor slowly pull her out and hand her off to the nurse. I remember hearing the loud "*WAH WAH WAH*" as my niece announced her entry to the world.

Tears were streaming down Marguerite's face, and Dave was grinning from ear to ear. I remember leaning over the side of my sister's bed, grabbing her hand and squeezing it as I said, "Good job!" I couldn't believe that this little life had been growing inside my sister for the past nine months, and now that my niece was born, I was an auntie.

By the time my niece was born, I started working even harder to change my life around. Up until 1996 and even a few years beyond, I was still grappling with depression, suicidal ideations, and self-harm. There were times where I was in and out of the hospital and I was so doped up on medication that I was almost unable to walk, or even think coherently.

In Samantha's first few years, I lived in Windsor and spent a lot of time with her. I would babysit her when her parents were working, would walk her to school and pick her up from school. I loved playing with her and watching her grow. I tended to spoil her from the time she was born. Every month she turned older, I bought her clothes or a little toy. She had my heart completely. When her parents split at the time she was three years old, I worked to make my role as an auntie pick up, but it wasn't without its faults.

I recall one time while visiting with her, I had got upset about something, and had taken more pills than I should have. I called her father at his work, and he very sternly told me to get myself to Emergency. After going to Emergency, and consequently being admitted for a few days, I called her father back, and said "They're releasing me, can I come back and stay?"

When he told me "no, you are not going to do something like this and be able to come back, like nothing happened," my eyes were truly opened to what I was risking—losing a relationship with my niece, and the loving support her father had always tried to give me despite his split from Samantha's mother, Marguerite. This came to me after a lot of thought, and of course therapy.

A lot of times, after I moved to Toronto, I felt a sense of guilt about leaving my niece behind, in pursuit of working on my healing journey, but her father had full custody of her, and I traveled back to Windsor every chance I got for her birthdays and the holidays. If I went travelling somewhere, I always tried to send something to her, just so she knew that I was always thinking of her.

When her father moved onto a new relationship, he continued to keep me in his life and hers, and that has meant the world to me, because essentially besides him, Sam and his ex, my sister Marguerite, I had no other family or support. A couple of years into Dave's new relationship, I became an auntie to two other girls, Madison and Dana. Marguerite also had moved onto another relationship and had another little girl, Alexandra. Sadly, due to familial troubles, and the ceasing of my relationship with my adoptive father, I haven't seen my other biological niece since she was five years old. Alexandra is now nineteen years old, and I often wonder if I will ever see her again.

The connection I have felt with Samantha has only grown stronger over the years, watching her grow into a young woman. She comes to Toronto to visit me, and I go to visit her from time to time also. From the time of Samantha's birth, I have felt an immense amount of love for her and have been very protective of her. When she goes through hard times, I try my best to be there for her, and she has been there for me also. She is like the daughter I never had.

With my Mom at her house in Ashern, Manitoba.

ANOTHER JOURNEY HOME

It's early morning and the sun has just risen. My friend has just dropped me off outside of the departures at the Toronto Pearson International Airport. I'm about to embark on another journey home. I'm a bit nervous. My guts are finally calming down from the night before. The nausea isn't hitting me as badly now.

I am prone to anxiety attacks. My anxiety always hits me tenfold before a trip and it always makes me think the worst. A million thoughts and questions rush through my head like *What if I miss the plane?* or *What if I get sick on the plane?* or *What if the plane crashes?* These thoughts don't ease until I am on the plane, sitting in my seat and I finally feel the plane taxi down the runway. I hold my breath and brace myself for lift off. As the plane picks up speed I look out the window and see the airplane runway get smaller and smaller.

I am heading out to see my mom and her partner Jim. I'm proud of myself because this time I've booked and bought the ticket myself. It may seem trivial to some people that I bought this ticket on my own but for me it's huge. It shows my growing independence, my desire to spread my wings and declare myself competent to the trustee I was placed under almost thirteen years ago at the hands of a psychiatrist I no longer see.

For me to get out from under my trustee, I must show that I am capable of handling the monies that I make from my freelance work, and the monies he issues to me from my account with the Ontario Public and Guardian Trustee Office. He's given me eight hundred dollars. Over half of that has gone towards my ticket; the rest is meant to help me get by while I am away. I'm worried that I will mess up, and hope I will manage okay.

Whenever I travel, I carry a special stone with me. Sometimes I carry the stone clasped in my hand, and other times it is enclosed in a small leather medicine pouch that I wear around my neck. This stone isn't just any stone; it's a spirit stone. Etched into the top of the stone is a buffalo. The buffalo is my clan, and in teachings I have received, it represents strength and courage.

Before I head into the airport check-in, I automatically think, *I need my morning smoke.* A thin sheen of sweat breaks out on my forehead as I wrestle with my overloaded suitcase, backpack, and purse. I'd like to think that I don't need the cigarette, but in my head, I tell myself I need it. I jokingly tell others and myself that smoking is my last vice, but I know it goes deeper than that. My need for cigarettes is no longer a habit; it has become a crutch. I've known that for a long time. I light a cigarette when I'm having a morning coffee. I reach for one when I am out and about, and I grab one as soon as I experience any feeling I'm not comfortable with—anxiety, anger, you name it. A cigarette accompanies almost every feeling I have each day.

Standing on the sidewalk, I pull out a cigarette, and put it in my mouth. I feel the mugginess of the air around me as I stand on the sidewalk. I light my cigarette and breathe in. The nicotine hits my lungs and then I exhale. I finish my cigarette in a matter of minutes and crush it in the grey cigarette disposal unit. A waft of cigarette smoke follows me as I walk inside to go to the airport check-in. The huge clock on the wall says 7:00 a.m. I have time to kill, so I walk the length of the airport corridor and go to a small coffee shop. With my stomach gurgling, I don't think I can handle a coffee, but I grab a diet Pepsi and a donut anyways because I know I must try to eat something. I pull my suitcase to a nearby booth and sit down. I don't know how long I sit there, maybe a half hour, before I realize I'd better check in, and I stand up and throw my garbage out. Pulling my overloaded suitcase behind me, wrestling with the backpack I carry on my back, and shifting my oversized purse on my shoulder, I make it to the airport check in. I pull out my printed e-ticket and stand in front of a kiosk that says WestJet Airlines. I am drowsy and only half awake.

"Can I help you ma'am?" a cheery male voice breaks through the fogginess.

I look up.

"Yes sir," I say. "I need your help to get my boarding pass."

"No problem," says the air attendant standing before me. He takes the ticket from my hand and turns to the kiosk. I try not to let him see that I am checking him out. He's nice to look at. He's tall and well built. His hair, though short, is a shiny wavy black and tousled-looking. He has the kind of hair you would want to run your fingers through just to straighten it out a bit.

It takes mere seconds for him to punch in my information. As we're both looking at the computer screen before us, he notices that I have a middle seat.

"Do you want to see if you can change your seat ma'am?" he asks.

"Sure," I mumble.

He fiddles around for a minute.

"Oh, I'm sorry, this seat will have to do, there are no other seats available."

"No problem," I say and he flashes a big white smile while handing me my boarding pass. Grabbing the boarding pass out of his hand I say, "Thank you sir," and walk towards the boarding desk to check in my oversized suitcase. Two minutes later I walk to security. I know the drill. I pull out two white bins and set them before me. I'm trying to hurry because I can see the line up behind me. Reaching down into my backpack, I pull out my laptop case. I open the case and pull my laptop out and put it in the bin. Next, I put my backpack into the bin and pull off my jacket and shoes. My backpack and its contents take up one bin, so I pull out a second bin. *Oh goodness, this is so bloody annoying,* I think to myself. After pulling out the second bin and placing my jacket, shoes and keys into it, airport security waves me through. I walk through the grey doorway entry. No lights flash and no sounds come from the radar placed within the plastic doorway entry. I am through!

I retrieve my two bins and put everything back into their rightful places. As I walk away, I smile. There is a sense of calm because this is probably the first time I haven't set off the alarm at airport security. I walk to the boarding gate and not long afterwards I am on the plane, making my way to my seat.

As I settle into my seat and get comfortable, I don't look out the window too much even though having a window seat is what I like the most. For some reason I only glance out to see the jet propellers turning and then focus on what's going on with the people around me. I like to see people settling into their seats, talking to each other, pulling out magazines or talking to the flight attendants as they go up and down the aisle.

As the plane taxis down the runway and heads into the air, I smile. At last, I am on my way for another journey home. In my head, I was saying *Winnipeg and Ashern, here I come!*

The flight to Winnipeg went quickly. It didn't seem as long as my last trip, but maybe that's because I wasn't as nervous this time around. After disembarking from the plane, I followed the same routine I had done on my previous trip—gathering my bags together and heading over to the bus station, to make sure I booked my ticket to Ashern.

I spent my time in Winnipeg this time by heading to Polo Park and this time I didn't get lost heading there. Malls are dangerous for me, just like for anyone else who likes to shop! While at Polo Park, I bought some little things that I didn't necessarily need, but it felt good to be walking around and popping in and out of the stores, just killing time.

After a while though, I started getting nervous, because I wanted to head back to the Greyhound bus station before it got too dark. With my shopping bags in hand, I made my way out to the bus stop, and stood there for about five minutes before the bus pulled up in front of me and a handful of people. I got onto the bus and made sure I sat right in the front, so I could see where I had to hop off.

Upon arriving back at the Greyhound bus station, I made me way to the locker that held my suitcases, and after wrestling with the lock for a second, I pulled out my suitcase and put my shopping bags in with the rest of my things. I sat down not far from my locker and started texting a couple of friends. Connecting with friends while on my travels always helped ease some of my anxiety.

The bus station was rather busy, and people were walking all around me, with their children in tow. Feeling some hunger pangs, I bought a couple of snacks from the snack machine—a Kit Kat bar, some chips and a Diet Coke. I munched on my snacks, and texted back and forth with friends in Toronto until it was time to board my bus.

This time, I couldn't get a seat close to the front, so I ended up at the very back of the bus, right where no one wants to sit—by the bathroom. I felt beyond tired, but knew if I fell asleep, I might miss my stop—Ashern. I kept myself awake by playing games on my phone, and in between that, trying to make sure that I heard every stop called.

When the bus driver finally called out ASHERN... I felt butterflies in my stomach because I was finally going to see my mom and her partner Jim again. After carefully making my way to the front, I peered out the door, and saw my stepdad's old grey truck idling at the side of the bus. There was something comforting about seeing his truck there every time I visited and needed to be picked up. It made me feel loved and wanted. I would be in Ashern at almost midnight every time I visited, and despite the fact my mom and her partner always headed to sleep early in the evenings, they would be there waiting for me.

My mom would get out of the truck, and silently come up beside me. I would give her a hug, and after my suitcase was put in the truck, we would head off to her house. After I settled in we would sit together at the kitchen table. I would have a coffee while she would sip at her tea. Sometimes, there were few words spoken, but the company made me feel like I was at the top of the world.

My Uncle Peter.

VISITING THE REZ

When I visited my reserve for the first time, my eyes were opened to how conditions in remote areas can lead to such feelings of helplessness and despair. Seeing my reserve was the first time I had seen a reserve other than Georgina Island on Lake Simcoe just outside of Toronto, Ontario. What I saw on Georgina Island was a far cry from what I was witnessing in Northern Manitoba.

Georgina Island is the First Nation I went to and learned to relax. I would sit around chatting with friends, or walk down to the water's edge to sit and bask in its tranquility. I would look to the sky and see the birds flying high, and witness ducks floating lazily by me, while sitting in deep thought and pondering things I didn't have time to while in the city.

My reserve, Peguis First Nation, is the largest First Nations community in Manitoba, with a population of approximately 7,200 people of Ojibway and Cree descent. It is located 190 km north of Winnipeg, Manitoba, Canada.

My first trip to Peguis First Nation was around 2013, and it was a spur-of-the-moment decision that my mom made. "Ah," she said, "we'll go to the rez, walk around, visit the band office, and maybe see if your Aunt Shirley and Uncle Sam are around."

I remember how excited I got.

That day my mom took me to the reserve for the afternoon, my uncle Pete picked us up. He had driven into Ashern and was there at 10 a.m. My mom's house is off the main highway in Ashern, but far enough removed that when a car drives up, the noise is almost welcomed because it breaks the quiet. Uncle Pete had honked his car horn while driving up my mom's driveway. I was rushing around gathering my things. Everyone who knows me knows that I don't go anywhere without my purse packed to the brim. I must have a Diet coke with me, pens, writing books, something to read, my iPod, my phone and a pack of smokes.

My mom was pulling on her coat. She glanced over at me.

"Are you ready?"

"Yeah almost."

"What?"

Ah crap! Sometimes I forget that my mom is hard of hearing and that I have to speak quite loudly in order for her to hear me properly.

"Yes, almost," I said a tad louder, and smiled.

I reached over onto the coffee table and grabbed my camera. I threw it in with the pile of stuff in my purse. I was tired and yawned the biggest yawn I could. I bet my mom saw my tonsils from where she stood. It was the mother of all yawns!

There was a bang on the back door of my mom's house. My mom's dog Duffy started barking.

"BE QUIET!" I yelled.

Two seconds later, I heard the creak of the back door opening and the stomping of feet coming up the back stairs. There stood my uncle, but he wasn't ready to leave. He wanted something to eat.

"Is there any food?" he asked, as he looked at us both.

My uncle was always hungry. His appetite astounded me. He could out-eat any one of us any day and I thought my mom had a huge appetite. My mom stopped pulling on her coat.

"Do you want some bologna?" she asked.

"Sure," said Uncle Pete. He ambled over to the kitchen table and sat down. My mom walked over to the fridge, and after a few seconds of fumbling around, she pulled a huge stick of bologna out. She held the stick of bologna in one hand, and some bannock in the other.

"Oh, that looks good!" my Uncle Pete says. "But don't make the sandwich as big as you did for Sam the other day."

They both laugh.

"Nah I won't," Mom says.

Apparently, when my mom had tried to make a sandwich for my Uncle Sam, she had cut the bologna so thick, it stood an inch high, and it had been too much for my other uncle to eat alongside the generous slice of bannock my mom had given him. They had all had a good laugh about that incident.

Uncle Pete gulped down his impromptu bologna and bannock sandwich, and we left the house. Road trip! We piled into my uncle's car. My mom was riding shotgun, and I was in the backseat. The seats were worn and old-looking and there was an overflowing abundance of papers on the seat beside me. I could smell cigarettes that had previously been smoked by God knows how many people who had sat in the seat before me. I saw my uncle's hand reach over to the radio and turn it on. Country music soon filled the car. The speaker beside me was working overtime because I felt it thumping against my leg. Uncle Pete wasn't saying much, and neither was my mom. I leaned over and asked, "Is there a way we can get some Tim Horton's coffee?"

My uncle started laughing, and then my mom started too.

"You can't get Tim Horton's coffee anywhere here," Uncle Pete said. "Unless you drive into the city."

Okay, so it was my first time going to the reserve, and I felt my cheeks turn fifty shades of red. My naive question really showed how much of an urban Native I was. I thought Tim Horton's was available everywhere, even on my reserve! Alas, I had to go without.

The road to my reserve is not paved like the city streets I am used to. It is a gravel road full of potholes and the occasional sinkhole. While driving you leave a plume of dust behind you. To avoid damaging their cars, drivers must often swerve to get past the holes. As I sat in the backseat of Uncle Pete's car, feeling every bump we hit, and watching the dust left in our trail, I thought of the game Grand Theft Auto, and how the character drives various cars. If you can't handle driving the getaway car, the car swerves all over the road. My uncle is not a bad driver, so I laughed at myself comparing driving on a desolate road to my reserve to this video game.

It was impossible to sleep in my uncle's car, what with the music blaring, the bantering back and forth between Uncle Pete and my mom, and the bumps that would jar me awake if I dared to nod off. About an hour later, we pulled up into Peguis First Nation. The first thing that greeted us was the worn sign that said, "Welcome to Peguis First Nation." A few minutes later, my uncle pulled up in front of a single-story building that housed the Peguis First Nations community mall, a Safeway store, health care office, bank, and band office.

I remember my mom and I getting out of the car and my mom turning and saying to him, "We'll be back in a few minutes." Off we went while Uncle Pete stayed in his car. My mom went in one direction, and I went in the other because I was anxious to see what was there. That was the first time I stepped onto the land my people call home. The people I met as I wandered around were warm and friendly but the vast land around me felt cold and uninviting. The winds blew, and patches of snow dotted the land everywhere around me. I remember the winds howling and the cold had me shivering and trying to burrow deeper into the thin coat I wore. The trees on the lands around the community hall stood tall and bare. They were like sentry guards, tall and foreboding. Later I did some research and found out that the trees on my reserve were either trembling aspen, white birch, or balsam poplar. They are the most common deciduous species in northern Manitoba.

As I walked, there was barely anyone around except for the occasional rez dog that roamed the area beside the Band Office. I could hear the SNIP, SNAP of the three flags as the wind hit them high up on their flagpole. A little while later, as I stood outside the mall entrance, I got my first look at what my reserve was like. I was totally unprepared for it. I saw wealth on one side of the reserve. There was a brand new Health Centre, a new school, and brand new houses for the teachers and RCMP detachment. On the other side, I saw desolation and poverty. There was a worn-down apartment block with grey concrete floors, dim yellow lighting and some broken windows. It was like a small city, but all jammed together in an uninviting parcel of Crown land.

Sometime while I was happily looking around at the Band Office or wandering around the only grocery store, Uncle Pete had driven off. I didn't know until then that his car was a Nish taxi. My mom and I met back up again at the front entrance of the mall, and decided to walk to the apartment block to look for my uncle. It was bitter cold, and I remember the cold seeping through my jacket and making me shiver. I wasn't used to this climate, and asked myself *what kind of Native am I if I can't handle this type of weather?*

My mom and I walked for about ten minutes, but it felt a lot longer than that because of the cold. As we walked, the abject poverty I witnessed was staggering, almost overwhelming. There was the brand new school and a brand new Health Centre, and empty house frames where the reserve officials said new houses would be built. Not far from them was the run-down apartment block. Housed next door to the community's hall were the VLT machines, where I noticed people sitting, feeding the machines for hours at a time. This first journey home revealed many things to me. It told me truths that not many people want to hear or speak of. It spoke of poverty, loss, and desolation. It spoke of sadness, anger and kindness; but also, of a resiliency that made me proud.

Apart from residential schools, the next worst thing that the Canadian government did was to remove First Nations children from their birth families and adopt them out. My siblings and I were taken from my mom as toddlers. I learned that the years that ensued after that consisted of my mom just trying to get by in any way she could. She lived in poverty, dealt with mental health and addiction issues, struggled with diabetes, and now was trying her best to be a mom to me even though she had grown up without her own mom. In a story I overheard between my mom and Aunt Shirley, I learned that when my mom was just twelve years old, she had been told by her mom, my grandma, to go to the store to pick up some milk. My mom went to do this errand, but when she came back, she found my grandma on the floor. She had been murdered during an argument with her sister. Not long afterwards, my mom was taken to residential school. While away at residential school, her father, my grandpa, also passed away, but the residential school my mom was attending at the time would not allow her to leave to go to the wake or funeral. The schools my mom attended were Birtle Residential School and Brandon Residential School. I am not sure which one refused to let her attend her father's funeral.

The stories I heard while back home spoke to the colonial practices and policies that have been carried out by the Canadian government. I listened to stories that detailed the loss of language, culture and tradition, and the ensuing estrangement of family members, the onslaught of addiction issues, the prevalence of diabetes amongst family members, and death. I was told about so many deaths that it made my head spin. There was the car accident that took a cousin away before his time. I believe he had only been in his twenties at the time, and though I spoke to him a couple of times after making contact with my aunt Shirley, my memories of the conversations I did have with him have become fuzzy. There was the murder of my maternal grandmother at the hands of her own sister, the deaths of my grandfathers, and the murder of my biological father.

During this trip I visited my community's graveyard, where my mom and her partner pointed out where family members were buried. We went to the neighbouring reserve, Fisher River First Nation and I also walked around that cemetery, looking for where my dad and my grandpa were buried. At one point, I thought I found where my dad was buried, but it turned out to be someone else's grave. Inside my head, I was praying, "Please Creator, help me to find the graves I am looking for." After going to the Band Office, and making a couple of phone calls, I met two of my uncles, who showed me where my grandpa was buried. One uncle brought me back to his apartment to show me family photos, and then graciously allowed me to take a couple of them with me. The kindness shown to me at that time totally blew me away. It reminded me of a gentle kindness that was often shown to me by the workers who took care of me while I was growing up.

****

Establishing a relationship with my birth mom was difficult at times but it was also rewarding. It was unique in the sense that I was getting to know her after so many years of not knowing who or where she was, and she was learning about me too. In many ways, the role of mother/daughter was reversed for us because during my visits I was often watching out for her, giving her advice, and making sure that overall, she was okay, just like I would when I was around my niece.

One day we had all gone into town to the Support Centre to hang out and my mom took off to get a haircut. When she didn't return after an hour, her partner Jim and I went looking for her. She had gone MIA. I remember my heart going into my throat, and the worry I felt when she had not returned after an hour. I went into the salon, and they told me, "Anna left a while ago."

I went across the street to two other places she usually went to and found that she wasn't there either. Her partner and I hopped into their truck and returned home. After entering the house, calling her name, and realizing that she wasn't anywhere to be found, we hopped back into the truck and drove back down the main street, keeping our eyes peeled for her. About an hour after my mom had gone MIA, we drove down Main Street, and slowly passed by the Co-Op store in case she was inside. We found her not long afterwards, at the back of the grocery store picking through the garbage for cans. After her haircut she had decided to collect cans that she could turn in to make a bit of money.

There were other incidents that had me on guard and vigilant around her, and it was disheartening to witness my mom's mental health deteriorate each time I was there visiting. Her partner watched out for her too. He had told me that after taking her to the doctor's, he'd learned she had been diagnosed with Tourette's. I don't know what mental condition my mom suffered from besides depression, anxiety and diabetes, but I never believed the doctor's diagnosis of Tourette's. It wasn't like she was showing the signs of the disease—at least the ones I had looked up on the computer such as the outbursts of swearing, and limbs flailing. It made me feel sad that my mom was in the shape that she was in, but I was also immensely proud of her because after all that she had been through, she still showed a resiliency that said, "I will not be destroyed."

I am proud of my mom. I feel a love for this woman who birthed me and who welcomed me back after all the years we were separated. Her resiliency has helped me to keep on fighting the good fight to create the change that is needed for the generation behind me to pick up and carry on.

My Uncle Sam.

Road trip with my sister Marguerite (left).

ROAD TRIP WITH MY SISTER

I'm about to embark on a three-day road trip with my sister Marguerite and her partner Jeff. The anxiety is bubbling up inside me. I've been anxiously waiting for a text message or a call from my sister to tell me that she and her partner have hit the road and will be arriving in Toronto soon. As soon as they hit Toronto, I am hoping we'll hit the road to head home to Ashern.

Marguerite and her partner live in Windsor, which is a four-hour drive at the best of times to Toronto where I've lived for almost twenty years. I'm pacing back and forth in my apartment. Each passing minute makes me more anxious than the last. My phone has rung a couple of times, and each time I jumped because I am expecting it to be my sister. This time, it's no different, here it goes again.

RING… RING… RING…

RING… RING… RING…

"Hello?" I say. It's my friend Jackie.

"Are you all packed?" she asks me.

"Yeah, I am. I'm just waiting to hear from my sister now," I reply.

Jackie and I talk for a few more minutes. Then she says, "You sound tired, Christine, maybe you should rest for a bit."

"Yeah, I guess I should, I've been awake since dawn," I say.

After a few more minutes of chatting, I hang up, and head towards my bed. No sooner do I lie down on my bed when my phone makes a shrill whistle, signaling a text message. I pick it up, squinting at my phone screen. It's a text from my sister. It says:

> We have to go to Canadian Tire
> to get a part for our truck. We'll be
> delayed…

Laying on my stomach, with my phone in front of me, I text back as fast as I can.

> Ok. How long are you going to be
> delayed?

> I don't know, depends on if we can get the part right away.

> Alright

I think to myself, *Damn I just want this trip to start.*

****

I get up and pace back and forth again. I repeatedly check my luggage, repacking and reshuffling things around in my bag to make things more compact. When I'm not fussing with my luggage I play with my cat Teddy. I'm not sure what to take with me because my sister had told me that on the way to Manitoba, we might go camping. The diva in me was on high alert. I knew that what I had in my suitcase was probably not suitable for camping—books, sketch book, beading materials—but I wanted to bring them anyways. My motto has always been "take everything you can" and boy, do I ever put that motto to good use.

As I'm waiting for Marguerite and Jeff, I realize that I have never really been on a road trip with anyone, so heading back home with my sister and her partner is kind of a big deal. Not only is it the first time that my sister is meeting our birth mom, but it's also the first time since we were children that I am spending more than just a few hours with my sister. Questions swirl around my head. *Are we going to get along, okay? Will we drive each other crazy?*

For the next couple of hours, I do what I can around my apartment. I make sure the dry and wet cat food is out for my friend who is going to come in and take care of Teddy while I am away. I also make a quick trip to the dollar store down the street. I figure what the heck, I might as well get some snack food for the first leg of the car ride. I lug my bag back from the Dollarama and place it beside my other luggage. I want to take a nap, but my nerves are shot. I sit at my kitchen table, listen to some music from my computer, and play a few video games. Doing this takes up most of my time, and soon my phone whistles shrilly.

I grab my phone. It's another message from my sister.

> We're on the road, we'll be there in the late afternoon or early evening.

> Yay!

I can feel my nerves begin to calm a little bit. My stomach isn't in knots. They're on their way! I go to lay down for a bit, knowing that some sleep will pass the time. I hit my bed, and no sooner do I lay my head down, I fall asleep. My dreams are fitful but at least I'm sleeping.

Suddenly, I hear the muffled sound of my phone ringing RING… RING… RING…

I jump up from my bed and fumble for my phone. Without my glasses on, I can't locate it right away, but after tossing a couple of pillows out of my way; I find my phone hiding under a book. I grab it, squint at the screen, and realize it's my sister. As I answer it, I shove my glasses on.

"Hello?" I say.

"Hey! We're nearly there so get your stuff ready. We're parking in McDonald's. Then we'll come to meet you," she says.

"Okay," I reply

McDonald's is just a stone's throw away from my apartment building. Another twenty minutes pass. I am getting my stuff lined up at the door, and my phone whistles again. It's another text message.

> We're here, but we have to organize the truck to make room for you lol. Jeff will come to get you and help you with your luggage once we're finished.

Having had enough delays, I put my light windbreaker on and grab my bags. I don't bother waiting for them to come and get me. Instead, I pull all my bags out into the hallway of my apartment and start lugging them to the front exit. It doesn't matter that they weigh a ton or that it's raining outside, I pull all my luggage out of my building and down the street to the parking lot of McDonald's.

When you live in a basement apartment, you don't always get to see how bad the weather really is. I don't realize just how much the rain is pelting down until I step out the door, so I stop for a second and pull my windbreaker a little tighter around me. A bag starts to tip over, I swear under my breath... Damn it!

With one hand, I pull up the bag that is falling, and with the other I try to pull up the hood on my windbreaker. It doesn't do any good, it falls back down the minute it hits my head. I stop again, and this time yank my sweatshirt hood up. I start to walk even faster, as the rain pelts down around me. I'm pulling one suitcase, carrying a backpack on my back, have a purse over one shoulder and another bag that I have somehow fashioned to fit over my suitcase handle. The bag over my suitcase handle holds a pillow and a blanket. *I don't need any help with my stuff, I think to myself.*

After a five-minute walk, I've arrived in the McDonald's parking lot. Though it is a bit darker than usual because of the cloudy skies and rain, through my rain splattered glasses, I see my sister and Jeff pulling things out here and there from the back seat of their truck and hear them bicker back and forth.

"No, don't put that there! That bag belongs here," my sister says

"Why? It makes more sense to put it here then to have it go there," Jeff replies.

I hear my sister say again, "Put the bag right there!"

I hear an oomph... escape from Jeff's mouth as he maneuvers a couple more bags in the back seat of their white Ford Avalanche truck. Then I yell, "Hey!"

Marguerite and Jeff turn around, and say, "Hey, we would have helped you with your bags."

"Nah," I say. "I got tired of waiting, so I thought I would make it easier by bringing my stuff out."

"Well, it's raining like crazy. We would have gone to get you," my sister says, looking at all my bags. "Oh geez, you have a lot of stuff!" She lets out a laugh that can be heard throughout the whole parking lot.

"Hmmph..." Jeff grunts as he moves another bag. As he's moving bags around, he looks back and sees my stuff.

"HOLY Chrissy!" he says. "You think you have enough stuff?" He looks at my suitcase, my backpack, another bag that I have packed to the hilt and my purse. He laughs, and as he's laughing, he stops long enough to pull out a cigarette.

"Oh, whatever!" I say to Jeff as I instinctively pull out my smokes too.

As I pull a drag on my cigarette, the wind from the rain hits me full force and my umbrella flies inside out, soaking my cigarette instantly. If the wind had been any stronger, I would have looked like Mary Poppins flying! So much for that cigarette. I drop it on the ground where it is immediately soaked up by the rain puddle it lands in. I grab my umbrella and fold it back to how it's supposed to be, being careful not to let the spokes poke me.

We all stand there for a couple of minutes and as Jeff finishes his cigarette, he grabs my bags to put them in the truck. He looks at one bag and sees that it contains a blanket and a pillow.

"Oh, you can leave that one here, Chrissy," he says.

"Why?" I ask.

"We have blankets for you," my sister pipes in.

"Well," I say "I'm bringing my pillow with me because I made it especially for the trip."

"Oh, ok," my sister replies. "But take that blanket back to your apartment."

"Fine," I say. I grab the bag, yank the pillow out and walk towards the truck. I pull the door open and throw my pillow in before I turn around and slam it shut again. I grab the bag with the blanket in it and head back to my apartment. The rain is making me angry, but I keep my sweatshirt hood up and walk as fast as I can.

Five minutes later, after fumbling at the gate of my apartment building, I run to the front door, put my key in, and step inside the door. I take a deep breath, walk down the hallway, and open the door to my apartment. I place the bag inside the door, say bye to my cat one more time and then lock up again.

Once again, I make my way to the McDonald's. By the time I reach the truck, my sister and Jeff have organized everything and are ready to put my things in. I hop into the backseat of the truck, while Jeff heads into McDonald's to get us all a meal. He comes out five minutes later and we chow down. Ten minutes later, radio blaring and making ourselves as comfortable as possible, we are off.

The road trip has commenced. YAY!

The road trip with my sister and her partner had its ups and downs. When we first took off, we all spoke animatedly with each other, basically catching up from the last time I had seen them. That had been maybe about three months before our trip. I asked my sister if she was nervous about meeting our mom. She didn't let on that she was.

While my sister is famous for never speaking about her feelings, I am the total opposite. I attribute that to the years of therapy I have had, but also to a fear of making my sister angry in any way. As the youngest sister, I was always somewhat of a peacemaker when my sister and I had any kind of conflict. I often felt that I had to walk on eggshells around my sister because she was quick to anger, and if my voice changed in the slightest, she would ask "Why are you talking that way?" or "What's wrong with you?" Often I preferred to stay silent if I thought she was being loud, if she seemed upset, or if she was bickering with her partner.

The first part of the trip was rather uneventful. Sitting in the backseat of their truck, I found myself often pushing luggage aside, so that it wouldn't fall onto me. Our first stop was at a rest stop in Barrie. We all kind of tumbled out of the truck, stretched our legs, and went in to use the washrooms and grab some food. It was all greasy fast food, but I remember impatiently standing in line at one of the places, squinting at the menu screen, contemplating what I wanted, even though I already knew I wanted a nice big whopper and fries.

After we all had grabbed our food, and had a cigarette, we headed back to the truck and hopped in. I ate my burger quickly, carefully making sure that I didn't make any mess, and slurped down my diet coke. After we had our food, we got back on the road again. We seemed to stop every three hours or so, but when it got dark, after Marguerite called about motel vacancies, we would pull into a motel, and tiredly bring some of our belongings into the motel room with us.

Often, we would have a few beers, maybe more, and then retire for the night. I loved having a Queen or King bed to myself, because it was reminiscent of being back in my own bed in Toronto. There is something about travelling that makes me miss the comfort of my own bed. Travelling with my sister made me miss my independence because I often felt relegated back to being the little sister and missed making my own decisions and going at my own pace. Marguerite seemed to be the one who called the shots for everything we did.

After staying in about three to four different motels on our way to Winnipeg, we were all excited when we finally made it to the border of Ontario and Manitoba. Greeting us at the border was a huge double rainbow. We stayed at one more motel and the next day, gathered our things, repacked the truck and headed into Winnipeg. Our drive through Winnipeg was fairly quiet aside from the music pumping out of the truck's speakers. Driving into Ashern didn't take too long, but I was excited and nervous for my sister. But I soon found out I had nothing to worry about. My stepdad Jim stepped outside before Mom.

"Anna!" he called. "Your daughters are here."

When my mom came outside to meet us, I remember her face twitching, but she reached out to Marguerite and they hugged like they already knew each other. I tried to videotape the reunion, but my recording didn't turn out—the battery had died.

That trip home was a bit more difficult than usual. Even though I initially stayed at my mom's house, an argument ensued when my stepdad got angry about me spending too much time with someone I had met. In the middle of the trip, after he and I had words on the phone, I went to stay in the motel room that my sister had. I left in haste, and my suitcase was left in my mom's house. I wanted to go back and get it, but Jim wouldn't let me. Soon after, he came to the motel room and an altercation happened between the two of us. He suddenly pushed me and I pushed him back. Marguerite was furious at him.

"Don't ever lay your hands on my sister," she yelled at him. It was the first time in quite some time that I had seen this protective side of Marguerite come out.

I felt badly about the situation with Jim, but I was also bullheaded about the whole situation too. Later I saw his truck circle around the little town a couple of times, then my stepdad pulled his truck into the motel parking lot. My mom was sitting beside him in the truck. Tears were rolling down her cheeks. I opened the truck door and reached over and gave her a hug. and then my stepdad got out of the truck and walked over to where we all were, outside of our motel room, having a couple of beers.

"Why don't we all just get along?" he said. He invited the guy I had met to join us, even though I knew he didn't really want him there.

After a get-together that night in my mom's backyard, and a couple of beers, I gathered the courage to apologize to my stepdad. A couple of days later, Marguerite, Jeff and I packed our stuff back into the truck and headed out for a week of camping. On our way to Riding Mountain, we came across the most beautiful scene. At first we saw a couple of bears off in the distance and then a herd of buffalo. In fact, traffic was stopped on this desolate road where we saw the buffalo. It took my breath away to be so close to two of my favorite wild animals. I don't recall much else about our camping trip, but when we did head back to Ashern, things were better between my stepdad and me, and my mom was relieved about that.

Overall, it was a road trip that I will never forget. I just wish that there hadn't been the drama with Jim. It was the last time that Marguerite and Jeff went to visit.

I went to visit my mom after that, but it wasn't the same because both my mom's and Jim's health had declined quite a bit, and they were no longer able to stay in their home. Instead, they were living in the hospital, and I stayed in a little motel across from the hospital that both my mom and Jim were staying in instead of at my mom's house. My mom had stomach cancer and Jim had had a massive stroke and couldn't take care of himself anymore.

IS THIS GOODBYE AGAIN?

This question kept going through my mind as I prepared for my trip back home. It was difficult not to cry. My birth mom had stomach cancer and her partner Jim had had a stroke.

I'd been calling the hospital every week for a month to get updates on how they were doing. Doctor Ehmadi told me my mom's condition was serious. She was in palliative care. I inhaled sharply. I hed to head back home to see my mom in a way I had never seen her in before. Just thinking about it made me sad. I wondered if my mom would hold on until I got there, or would she pass before I reached her bedside? She didn't deserve this illness. I asked myself, Why her?

My mom was kindhearted and generous. Through the years, she had sent me and my sister Marguerite monies to assist us when she could. She sent me birthday cards and Christmas cards, gave me little trinkets, told me she loved me, and called me every day. The phone calls meant the world to me, because even if we didn't have much to say to each other, we would both happily stay on the phone, and she would hum if the silence lasted too long. The humming would always make me smile. The Sixties Scoop took thirty years away from my relationship with my mom and it took forty-three years from her relationship with Marguerite.

The path to be reunited with my mom had been difficult. Eventually it led me to accept who she was and why she was the way she was—a woman of courage, strength and resilience. Now my mom was facing another challenge—cancer—and she was afraid. Not long after I learned about my mom's illness, her doctor told me I was needed at the hospital.

"We need you here to make some decisions," he said.

That statement made me panic. I'm in a different province, I'm under the care of a public trustee who takes care of my money, and I'm on government assistance. Now I'm being asked to go out to Ashern to make decisions for a mom I have only known for thirteen years.

What can I possibly decide for my mom? I wondered. *What can I do?*

I called a couple of friends and asked their opinion. Both of them told me: "This will be difficult, but your mom needs your help now."

I needed to go to Ashern to help my mom. I got off my butt and called my trustee, but I couldn't reach her on the phone, so I emailed her.

"My mom is quite sick, and they want me out there. Can I have the monies to visit? Please advise."

A day later, she wrote back:

"Christine, I'm sorry to hear about your mom. Of course, you can go out there. Please give me a roundup of the costs associated with this trip and I'll release the monies to you."

Sitting at my kitchen table, I called the hospital out in Ashern. I pushed auto-dial on the saved number in my phone list and listened to the silent space between the dial tone and the ring.

RING… RING… RING…

A garbled, but quiet voice, answered on the other end. "Lakeshore Hospital, how can I help you?"

"Hi, I'm calling to see how my mom is doing. Her name is Anna Smith. I also wanted to let you know I'll be coming to see her on January 20th," I say rather quickly. I don't like going through the nurses to find out how she is but I've quickly learned that my mom will never tell me how she is really doing. I guess it's because she worries I'll get upset, like I did before she went in the hospital. I had to practically beg her to go to see her doctor.

The nurse gave me a quick update. "Your mom is okay today. She's had some pain, but we gave her some medication for it. Other than that, she's just resting."

"Oh ok, that's good," I said.

I was expecting the nurse to hang up but she asked me, "Would you like to speak with your mom? We can put her on the phone if you'd like?"

"Sure!" I said and a few minutes later I heard my mom's voice come over the phone.

"Hello," my mom said loudly. Her breathing was a bit erratic and she cleared her throat.

"Hi Mom!" I said really loudly. We talked for a couple of minutes. I asked her how her pain was then asked a couple of other mundane questions like, "Whatcha doing?" and, "Did you eat your meals today?"

After she answered each question there was a brief silence and then I heard her start to hum.

"Mmmm mmmmm mmmmmm…"

"I'm coming out to see you soon," I said.

"When are ya coming out here?" she asked.

"January 20th."

"Ok," she said and started to hum again. "Mmmm… mmmmm… mmmmmm…"

I smiled listening to her

"I had better go, I just wanted to see how you were doing."

"I'm ok," she said.

"Ok then," I said. "I'll talk to you later."

"Ok," she said back.

"I love you," I said quickly.

"I love you too," she said.

A couple of seconds later, she hung up the phone and I listened to the dial tone for a second before I did too.

***

The trip is within a week and there's so much for me to do beforehand. I talk to a friend about looking after my cat. One friend agrees to stay at my place while I'm away, so I don't worry anymore about who's watching my cat. With that taken care of, I go about cleaning my apartment and doing laundry and then I go online to purchase my ticket for the flight home. The next week flies by in a hurry. I do everything that I need to do and then it's time for me to leave.

I pack my suitcase the night before my trip. I move back and forth between the two rooms of my apartment trying to figure out what I can take without over-packing for my week-long trip. I pick up books that I can read while away. I pick up my latest beading project, and wonder if I will have time to do it.

I look at my colouring books and pencils and stick them in the front of my suitcase. I pack my writing books. I know I'm bringing my laptop, there's no questioning myself over that one. I don't go anywhere without that piece of technology.

As I move between my suitcase and the wardrobe where I keep my clothes, my cat Teddy comes up to me and meows. I squat down beside him and pet him. He knows I'm leaving. I putter around for a couple of hours, picking up things, looking at them, and putting them away in their rightful spots. Because a friend is staying at my place while I'm away I want my place to be as tidy as possible.

Finally, I stop everything I'm doing and look at the clock. It says 10 p.m. *I guess I'd better get to bed*, I think to myself. I walk towards my window, pull the curtains a little closer together and then turn to my nightclothes that are already laid out on my chair. I strip from my usual attire of jeans, T-shirt and hoodie and pull on my worn-out jogging pants and thermal long-sleeved under shirt. From his perch on my bed, Teddy sleepily looks at me. I walk over to my nightstand and quickly gulp my medications down with a glass of water. I march to my bed and pull my duvet down. Before I lay down and cover myself up, I take my glasses off and lay them on the windowsill by my bed. I close my eyes.

Sleep doesn't come easily. I'm anxious and can feel my muscles tensing up. My heart is slightly racing, and I find I must do some quick breathing exercises. I slowly count 1… 2… 3… 4… and inhale and then exhale. I do this for about five to ten minutes. My meds start to take effect, and finally darkness overcomes me and I'm in dreamland. I don't sleep very long. As I shift my body under the heavy duvet that is covering me, I peer at my watch. It's only 3 a.m. I lay there and hope to God I fall asleep again. There's a weight on my legs and I look down and see Teddy sprawled over my legs. As I try to shift my legs, he awakens and glares at me as if to say, "How dare you wake me up!"

As I'm lying in my bed with my blankets around me, I am dreading having to get up at the god-awful hour of 5 a.m. Even though I have set my alarm for 5 a.m., I've been tossing and turning. I finally doze off at about 4:30, only to be awakened a half hour later by the annoying BEEP BEEP sound coming from my phone. It startles me for a few seconds and I hurriedly locate my phone by my bed and silence the alarm. Shaking the cobwebs out of my head, I throw my blankets off, swing my legs over the side of the bed and sit up. As my feet hit the floor, I cringe at the coldness that seeps through the floorboards and hits my toes. It's 5 a.m. and I must be at the subway for 6 a.m. and then the airport by 7 a.m.

I rush to the bathroom and lean over my bathtub to turn the hot and cold water taps on to take my shower. After struggling for a few minutes with my shower curtain coming off its hooks, I managed to get it back in order. I take my glasses off and place them on my sink and hop in for a fast shower. I lean my head backwards and feel the warm water wash through my hair and over my body. I blindly reach for the soap and start soaping myself up. Oh, how I love the smell of Zest soap! I could bask in its smell all day, but I only have a few minutes to shower and get myself ready. As I hurriedly wash the soap off, I think of the commercial jingle for Zest soap and sing it in an off-key tone.

I giggle as I turn the leaky water faucets off. The cold air hits me again and I shiver as I hurriedly wrap my towel around me and make my way back to my bedroom.

I had laid out my clothes the night before, so I didn't have to dig around my closet to figure out what clothes to wear. I had picked my favorite jeans (black of course), and a black T-shirt and hoodie. After getting my clothes on, I glance at the clock and notice it says 5:35 a.m. I have to rush through the rest of my morning routine. I make my bed, pet my cat and then quickly put my bulky Sorel boots on. I hate the boots, but I didn't know what kind of weather I would be heading into in Manitoba.

The beginning of my trip was a bit of a comedy of errors. First, I struggled to get my bags down to the St. Clair West subway station. I had to stop every few seconds to adjust my purse and backpack while still wheeling my suitcase down the sidewalk and onto the rickety escalator. Then I had to flash my metro pass and make my way through the turnstile and down another escalator only to realize that the most important escalator down to the subway was out of order and I had to manhandle my luggage down two sets of stairs. After that I had to take the subway all the way to Kipling and take the Rocket 192 bus to the airport. I managed to catch the Rocket 192 just in the nick of time. The ride was uneventful until we reached arrivals. Everyone else was getting off the bus, and I was so tired that I wasn't really paying attention and thought I also had to disembark to head into Pearson airport. As I struggled with my bags, I asked a fellow passenger if we were at Terminal 3. The lady, who was in a crisp navy-blue uniform, was probably either a flight attendant or worked somewhere in the airport. She said, "Dear, if you're going to terminal three, stay on this bus for a few more minutes because this is terminal one." I looked at her with relief and said, "Oh ok, thank you."

A couple of minutes later, the bus arrived at Terminal 3, and I whisked myself and my bags off and ran into the terminal. I fought my way through the crowd to the self-boarding kiosk. It wouldn't work for me. I tried to put my information in again, but it wouldn't work.

"You're past cut off time," an airline employee told me. "You need to get in line to check in."

Ah shit! The line up was long—too long, perhaps. I felt panic. I was breathing quickly and my heart was racing. I couldn't miss my flight! I must have made some type of face because the stewardess said, "Don't worry, I'll get you to the desk and through security."

"Oh, thank you!" I said, feeling a little relieved.

"Follow me" she said. As the stewardess made her way through the crowd, I quickened my pace. I was about to burst out laughing when suddenly, I saw her jump over the ledge at the desk. What agility! *I would have fallen flat on my face if I had tried that move*, I thought to myself. Smiling, I stood in front her while she entered my info and quickly looked over my passport. She handed me my boarding pass and said, "Come with me." She took off at a fast clip and I followed her until we reached security. She got me through the line and then said, "you'll make your plane, but you'll have to hurry as soon as you get through."

I thanked her once more and she left. A couple of minutes later I got through the airport checkpoint and then struggled to get my belongings back together, I ran to my gate. With a minute to spare, I reached it and saw I was the last one to board. *Phew!*

I quickly found my seat. I had a window seat and had to ask the two women in their seats beside me to move so that I could get to my seat. The woman beside me was grumbling because she had to move. She was clearly annoyed when I accidentally sat on part of her seatbelt.

"You're on my seatbelt," she said.

"I'm sorry," I said, as I shifted myself in my seat. I wanted to smack the dirty look she gave me off her face. Instead, I turned my head away and looked out the window. I watched the people on the tarmac in their bright neon safety vests, waving their arms and batons as other planes taxied in on other runways. I felt a jolt as the plane started to move. We taxied down the tarmac, and I braced myself for takeoff. I felt my muscles tense up and my hands clenched so tightly I could feel my nails dig into my palms. I'd been on planes before, but my nerves never settled down until we were actually in the air flying amongst the clouds.

Shortly after we took flight, I dozed off briefly, only to awaken a few minutes later to the feeling of my ears popping. The sharp pain of them popping made me cringe. I hated the feeling, but I quickly swallowed and felt them go back to normal. I stayed awake for a little while looking out the window to pass the time. I tried to stifle a huge yawn so that I wouldn't bother the lady beside me. But then I thought, *Who cares?* I felt my eyes growing heavy and soon I dozed off again.

I must have slept for the rest of the flight because when I awoke the flight attendants were going down the aisles telling everyone to turn off their electronics and prepare for landing. I braced myself for the landing. I was anxious to get off the plane. I felt claustrophobic from sitting so close to the passengers around me.

The plane hit turbulence. I tightened my grasp on the armrest as the plane got jostled like all of the mixed-up emotions I felt. How I wished I was going to visit my mom at her home, not in the hospital. I was not sure what to expect when I saw her, but the trepidation threatened the fake calm I wore like a mask upon my face.

We were only in the air for a few more minutes before I heard the pilot say, "Welcome to Winnipeg ladies and gentlemen. It is now 9:30 a.m." I quickly changed the time on my watch to 9:30, an hour behind Ontario. I took out my phone and took it off airplane mode. A bunch of beeping noises emanated from my phone as missed texts came through. I fumbled with my phone for a few seconds as I tried to turn the volume down. I shoved the phone into my pocket, so that my neighbour wouldn't glare at me or say something.

I stifled a yawn and grabbed my backpack from the floor. After a few seconds of standing in front of my seat, the ladies in my row moved forward, and I gladly escaped the confines of the small space I was stuck in between the planes wall and seat 14 F.

"Have a nice stay in Winnipeg!" the peppy flight attendant said as I exited the plane.

I smiled and kept walking. I wanted to get the heck off the plane! I walked down the tunnel into the airport, and followed the crowd to the baggage claims area.

I had a long layover in the airport. I found out via text shortly after I got to Winnipeg that my friend was unable to pick me up for a visit, so I hunkered down at the Tim Hortons by the exit and pulled out my phone. After about an hour I bundled up in my coat and made my way to the Greyhound station. Thank God it was not far because the cold was bone-chilling. It seeped through my coat, and boots.

It was a bit slippery because it was snowing and raining at the same time. I laughed at myself because I knew I was walking really slowly and shuffling my feet to make sure I didn't land on my butt on the sidewalk. The parking garage was dark with only a few streams of light coming through its sparse windows. The cars entering were few and far between, and it made the place that much more foreboding. I sped up, anxious to get out of the dark garage and into a warm building. I couldn't help but to think of my mom and wonder if her health issues were really as bad as I'd been told. Tears threatened to spill but I held them back. I didn't want to lose control in a public space. After a few minutes of struggling over the icy patches on the sidewalk, and managing not to fall, I reached the Greyhound station doors and pulled them open. Once inside I sat and waited for the bus, making myself at home in a corner of the station. I listened to my music and texted back and forth with one of my friends.

I did not arrive in Ashern until 2:30 a.m. on the Greyhound bus. It was an uneventful two-hour ride with many little stops in between, though I almost missed the ride altogether when I lined up for the wrong bus and was told to wait by the security guard at the doors of the Greyhound station. After that little mix up, the driver got me on the bus and watched where I sat down so he could easily locate me. I was nervous on the bus because I was scared that if I fell asleep, I would miss Ashern. I had been up since 3 a.m. the morning before.

I was glad that I had my iPhone because it meant that I would have better reception than the last time I had gone out to Ashern with a non-descript cheap phone that lost reception as soon as the bus reached Stonewall, Manitoba. My friend Katia and I were texting back and forth, and though it was pitch dark on the bus, that little bit of connection kept me calm. I checked Facebook a million times and my emails too. God forbid that I miss a post or an email! When I didn't have reception, I sat back and hoped the time would go by quickly.

The bus driver, though gruff with me in Winnipeg because I was the very last person to board his bus, was now being kind as he took my suitcase out from below the bus.

"You have a good weekend ma'am," he said.

As I grabbed the handle of my suitcase from the driver, I said "Thank you sir," and turned to start my trek to the little motel where I would be staying. A wave of sadness hit me. This visit was different from all my other ones. No one was there to pick me up like they were for my many other visits before. Both my mom and her partner Jim were in the hospital. Instead of going to my mom's house, I was heading to the little motel off the highway to stay. I never felt as lonely as I did in those moments when I got off the bus and headed over to the motel.

The next morning as I walked across the highway from the motel, the biting cold was seeping through my jacket. I shrugged and tried to draw my jacket in closer. I felt my stomach lurch just a little bit, and my eyes burned from the unshed tears I had been holding back since awakening. The walk to the hospital was a short one. As I reached the door, I took a deep breath before I walked in. I headed to the nurse's desk.

"I'm here to see Anna Smith" I told them. "I'm her daughter."

I was nervous about seeing my mom and as the head nurse led down the hallway to see her. Nothing had prepared me for what I would witness next. My mom was lying in her hospital bed and my stepdad Jim sat beside her in his wheelchair.

I sat quietly in the hard, plastic chair that was by my mom's bed. I was trying to stay strong in front of my mom, but it was so difficult not to break down. There was my mom, a shell of skin and bones. I knew that even though it may not happen during this visit, soon we would have to say goodbye.

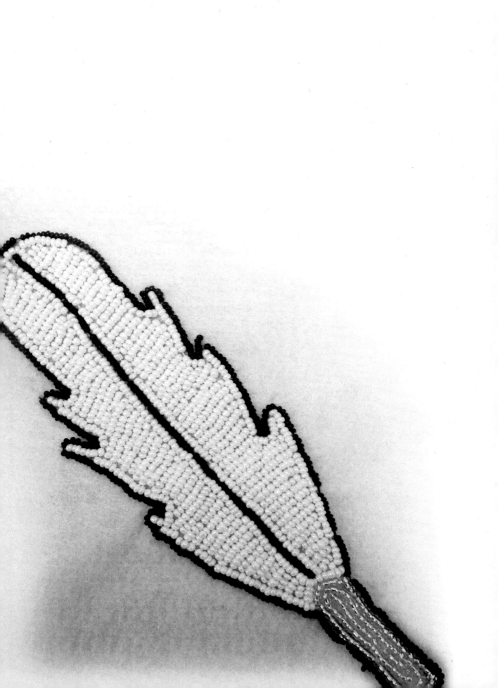

GONE

I remember that dream as though it happened yesterday. It's the one where I wake up short of breath and counting 1... 2... 3... in order to try and calm myself down. In the dream, I received a call saying, "Christine, I'm sorry—your mom has passed away."

I first had this dream at a time when I was a bit distanced from my mom. There was a period when I didn't talk to my mom for a bit, not because I didn't want to but because I wasn't sure how to handle having my mom in my life. It was through no fault of hers, nor mine. I wasn't accustomed to having a "mom" in my life. I know that may sound weird but nothing had prepared me for this relationship. When children are taken away from their families, cultures and traditions, due to the assimilationist policies of a colonial government, they really don't know how to act or behave when all of a sudden they are reunited. When I first re-established a relationship with my mom, it was very difficult. As time went on, I slowly learned how to interact with her, and also how to love her.

When I had that dream years ago, about receiving a phone call saying my mom had died, I didn't really think much about it at first. I thought it was just because of me and my fatalistic thoughts.

On August 25, 2017 I had an appointment with an employment counsellor at the place where I currently work in downtown Toronto. I was sitting in a chair just steps away from the front desk at Miziwe Biik Aboriginal Employment and Training Resource Centre, when my phone rang.

RING... RING... RING...

I had my earphones on because I was listening to some music on my iPod, but the shrill ring of my phone broke through and made me jump in my seat. Yes, I scare easily. Since my mom had become ill, every time the phone rang, and the area code 204 flashed on my caller id, I was scared of what it might be. Often, I wished that the hospital where my momma was staying would call and say, "Hey, your mom is better. She's going home." But that call never happened. After all, my mom was ill with stomach cancer and hadn't been home in months. Her last year had been spent in the hospital, and that thought alone always had me close to tears, even though I tried my best to stay composed on the outside. Inside, though, I was a mess.

On this day, when my phone rang, I practically ripped my earphones out of my ears, so that I could pick up my phone and answer.

"Hello, Hello?" I said breathlessly.

It sounded as though I had run across a room to answer the phone, but really, I had been sitting beside it.

"Hello?" a woman's voice said. "May I speak to Christine?"

I heard some muffled noises in the background around me and I was a bit distracted because my appointment time was coming up.

"This is Christine," I said quickly.

The woman on the other end of the phone told me she was the head nurse at Lakeshore General Hospital in Ashern. What the nurse said to me is a bit of a blur.

"Your mom is going downhill fast," she said. "She isn't breathing very well, and she isn't eating."

"Isn't there something you can do? Give her a feeding tube? Keep her going?" I said selfishly. I wasn't ready to let my momma go just yet. I had just been on the phone with her a few days before. "When are you coming to visit me again?" she had asked.

"I'm going to come to see you in the fall, Mom," I'd told her. "I can't afford to go out right now."

I had teared up when I told her that. Money was always an issue when it came to getting out to Ashern to see my momma. The cost of a flight, bus ticket, and motel stay was enough to sink me financially. I had to plan my visits strategically because I didn't have a place to stay other than at the motel that sat across the highway from the hospital where my mom was being treated.

It was quiet on the other end of the phone for about a minute before my Mom had answered.

"Ok, fall is good," she'd said. "Everything will be good in the fall."

I felt her disappointment, and knew she was trying to be strong. The resiliency and strength of my mom was amazing. We talked for a few more minutes that night. Before hanging up I told her, "I love you," and she told me, "I love you too."

After the call with my mom, I had my appointment with the employment counsellor and somehow after that appointment, I made it across downtown to go and see my friend Jen at the University of Toronto's First Nations House.

When I arrived I was distracted, trying not to think of the phone call I'd had with my mom two hours earlier. I tried to say hello to my friend and others around me in the cheeriest way I knew, but there was a heaviness inside me. I had taken my phone and placed it in the charging stand. I walked away from it for a bit. I had been sitting in the conference room in a worn-out black chair, staring kind of mindlessly at the chalkboard before me, when I heard my phone ringing once again.

I didn't want to answer it but there was a sense of urgency within me when I heard my phone that time. I tore across the floor from the conference room to behind the front desk. I fumbled clumsily but managed to answer.

My caller ID flashed with the name "Lakeshore General Hospital."

"Hello?" I answered.

The same nurse I had talked to two hours before was on the other end of the call. Before she could get the words out, I knew. My mom had passed away.

On August 25, 2017, at 3 p.m., my mom began her journey to the spirit world.

I was quiet for a second and then the tears came. My friend Jen saw my face crumple and the tears pouring down my face.

"It's ok, Christine. It's okay," she said. She led me back to the conference room and had me sit down. In a daze, I called my sister, and let her know. I called a couple of friends, and not long after that, I got up and headed back home.

It was raining that day. I walked home slowly, thinking of my mom.

"Why? Why did you have to go?"

At first, I was angry because she didn't make it to autumn so that I could go to visit her. I was also angry at the Children's Aid for robbing me of the years I could have had with my mom. But there was also an overwhelming sadness because I had lost the mom I had searched for over so many years, the mom I had yearned for my entire life. I couldn't call her anymore, couldn't hear her voice, couldn't tell her "I love you" one more time, or hear her say it back to me. Once again, I was left without a mom, and I felt like a lost child again. I not only had to grieve the loss of my mom, but I also had to grieve the lost years and what could have been.

Living without my mom has been difficult. There isn't a day that goes by that I am not thinking of her and wishing that she was still here. But I also know that my mom lived her life as long as she was able to. At times, her life had been full of pain and torment because she had survived and witnessed so much trauma. Some of the stories I had heard over the years I knew and spent time with her broke my heart. But despite it all she had found me, she had found my sister, and though at first the relationship between us had been tenuous; we had survived it and built a strong connection.

There are memories of her I will always hold onto. I think of our phone calls every day, of my yearly visits to see her, of going out to Ashern, and of taking care of her as much as I could while she was in the hospital. There will always be a part of me missing. She is no longer here physically and so I can't reach out to touch her. I can't give her a hug. I can't tell her what I most want to say.

"I love you, Mom."

I can honestly say I haven't been the same since my mom went on to the spirit world. But my mom was strong, and I understand that so much better now. Her strength inspires me to stay strong and to never give up. My mom never gave up and neither will I.

THE QUESTION OF HOME

One of the impacts of the Sixties Scoop on me as an individual is that it has always made me question the concept of home, and what it actually means. When I contemplate what home is, I think about my biological family, question the audacity of the Canadian government in taking my siblings and me from my mother, kidnapping us to another province.

It has taken me years and I'm still healing from that so-called family who adopted me as a toddler only to give me up and put me back into "care" at the age of ten. Being taken from your family, your community, your culture and traditions, and forced into the foster care system as a Crown Ward is something no child should have to go through. So many Indigenous children's lives have been destroyed by what the Canadian government did by enacting the assimilationist policies that they did.

Where is home I ask? I made Toronto my home after I moved here for treatment that literally saved me from an untimely death. I found my birth mother in my early thirties and I fought to establish a relationship with her because that is what I wanted the most.

Holidays and birthdays are challenging because I have often felt like I'm the one who is lost. I am an orphan and have been for years since my mother died. I can no longer call her or reach out to her. She was the glue that held me together in so many ways because I could finally say, "I have a mom."

I can't say that anymore though, and that hurts me to the core. It's a pain that never goes away. I'm so thankful that parts of her family have kept in touch with me, after I went to her funeral. It means more than they will ever understand. I feel like my mom is watching me from above.

Others have stepped in to help me to establish what home means to me. I thank the Toronto Indigenous community for giving me a community to belong to. I thank First Nations House at the University of Toronto which has been a "home" where I have been able to celebrate holidays and important events with my FNH "family." I thank the individuals I've met while I was fortunate to study at the University of Toronto, not only for my undergraduate degree but also my Master's degree.

Canada, you made me and countless other Indigenous children/people feel lost because you stole us from our homes and families, leaving us to wonder who we are and where we belong. Without community, culture and language, what connects and grounds us? Home—what is it? Where is it? These are questions that have often left me reeling and wondering if will I ever feel at home spiritually and emotionally.

My Mom's home.

THE HAPPIEST I EVER WAS

The happiest I ever felt was when I met my birth mom. I remember I had trepidation at first because I was unsure of how the meeting would go. I had waited years to meet her and learn who she was.

The first time I travelled out to Winnipeg to meet her, I went by Greyhound bus because that was what I could afford. I wasn't earning much at the time, and I was on Ontario Disability. But I didn't care—nothing could have stopped me from meeting my mother.

It took three long days to get there by bus, but it was worth it. As we got closer to the Winnipeg bus terminal, I turned around and excitedly told a random woman behind me that I was finally getting to meet my mom. The woman was happy for me, but that was also when I realized that not many people knew about the ramifications of adoption and what it can do to some people. She wished me good luck, and I thanked her.

I was trembling when I got off the bus, not only because it was cold, but because I was nervous and excited. I was finally getting to meet the woman who gave birth to me, the woman who gave me life. As I walked into the bus station and looked across the rows of seats, there stood a woman. She had thick glasses, wavy salt and pepper hair, and as our eyes met, she started to cry.

She reached out and awkwardly put her arms around me. At that moment I knew I had finally made the connection I had wanted to make all my life.

I was home.

SHORT STORY

by Christine Miskonoodinkwe Smith

A STEP BY STEP GUIDE TO ANNOYING YOUR TEENAGE DAUGHTER

Step One… You require a daughter, preferably your own and not someone else's. After all you could get murdered by the other girl's overzealous protective aunt.

She must be going through a case of raging hormones, moments of flightiness and attitude problems. The kind where, if she says another "OH WHATEVER" to you when you ask her to clean up after herself, you'll want to take your hands and wring her bloody neck.

Step Two… She must have lots of friends who come over on a regular basis. There's nothing like annoying your daughter amongst friends. After all, you believe it builds character.

You will play Stomping Tom Connor music and yodel right along with him in an off-key voice, while your daughter tries to yell over the music:

"MOTHER! YOU'RE EMBARASSING ME!"

Step Three… When your daughter least expects it, like when she is on the phone with her latest crush, decide to yell,

"You're out of deodorant and you need a new box of tampons!"

I mean why not announce to the world that your daughter has become a woman. It happened to you!

Step Four... When your daughter is about to leave with her friends, make sure you fawn over her, wipe at that stray piece of hair that you see covering her mouth, or take your finger, spit on it, and wipe that dirt mark you see on her cheek. Or better yet say,

"Dear, do you want me to clean your eyeglasses with my magic cloth? I don't want you to not be able to see where you are walking, you could trip and hurt yourself."

Step Five... This is the fifth and final step. Tell your daughter you'll take her shopping and when you're in the car, roll down all the windows, and blare your daughter's music. Promise her you won't sing but then as the rap music comes on yell:

"M to the O to the M! What does that spell?"

And then tell her:

"This music is sick!"

ABOUT THE AUTHOR

Christine Miskonoodinkwe Smith is a Saulteaux woman from Peguis First Nation. She is an editor, writer and journalist who graduated from the University of Toronto with a specialization in Aboriginal Studies in June 2011 and went on to receive her Master's in Education in Social Justice in June 2017. Her first non-fiction story "Choosing the Path to Healing" appeared in the 2006 anthology *Growing Up Girl: An Anthology of Voices from Marginalized Spaces*. She has written for the *Native Canadian, Anishinabek News, Windspeaker, FNH Magazine, New Tribe Magazine, Muskrat Magazine* and the *Piker Press*. She has also co-edited the anthology *Bawaajigan* with fellow Indigenous writer Nathan Niigan Noodin Adler.